Angel

Jamie Canosa

©Jamie Canosa 2014

Cover Design: KKeeton Designs
Cover ©Jamie Canosa 2014

ISBN-13: 978-1514783610

ISBN-10: 1514783614

One

If I had to choose a way to die, and asleep in my bed of old age wasn't an option, I think I'd choose drowning. It sounds awful, but I don't think it would be. There's a quiet to being under the water. A stillness you can't find anywhere else. Perfect peace as the world just fades away. It doesn't seem like such a bad way to go.

Breaking the surface, I sucked in oxygen, feeding my deprived lungs. The campus pool was usually deserted first thing in the morning, which made it my favorite time to swim. There was no comparison between the still water of the heated, indoor pool and the ocean. The rhythmic whoosh of waves breaking overhead, currents twisting and turning, tides pushing and pulling. The ocean is alive. It's a challenge for those willing to accept the dangers that come along with it. An adventure. One I used to thrive in.

But that was then. Now, I'd learned the value of peace. The blessing of that elusive stillness. Ironically enough, underwater felt like the only place I could catch my breath.

The slap of my hands on the cold tile echoed through the cavernous space as I lifted myself from the water. A navy towel sat, folded, on the bleachers beside my shirt and sandals, which I used to scrub the chlorine from my hair.

A shower would have been nice, but if I didn't stop by the library to pick up research materials for the paper I had due in Social Sciences, I'd never get around to actually writing the thing. My venture into the campus library the week before had been a bust. Picked clean. Which left me no choice but to swing by the local branch on my way home. Soggy trunks and all.

***

The librarian on duty was an older woman. If I had to guess, I'd say . . . late sixties? But, with her silvery hair tied back in a bun tight enough to stretch the sagging skin around her eyes and a serious stick up her ass, she may have been the most formidable person I'd ever met. Icicles formed in her glacier blue eyes, aimed directly at me over the top of her half-moon glasses, as I trailed water droplets across the worn green carpeting.

I wasn't planning to stick around long enough to make a puddle, but the reference section was a joke. Even with all *three* aisles fully stocked, there wasn't much to choose from. Not that I knew *what* I was choosing, anyway.

Side effects of the 'human condition'. That was the paper topic. And literally *all* I had to go on. Torturing students with incredibly vague paper topics for one's own amusement, was that a side effect? No, probably not. But insanity had to be.

I scanned book after book, seeking . . . inspiration. I was running out of time. I needed to make a damn decision and get things rolling. After sorting through a shelf and a half, it occurred to me that there was no rhyme or reason to the way things were organized. If I had any hope of leaving there with any sort of direction in mind, I was going to have to run it through the catalog.

A faint tapping led me to a dusty bank of computers in a dim corner behind the nonfiction titles. Not many people used public computers anymore, but a pale, thin girl with mousey brown hair sat hunched over a keyboard, hammering away at the keys. Not a flattering description, but there was something about her that was . . . remarkable. I think it was her eyes. She had the most intense blue eyes I'd ever seen. Darting back-and-forth across the screen, it was more than just concentration I saw in them. There was fear and pain and sadness. But beneath all of that there was this light. This tiny flickering flame, fighting to stay lit.

I was a moth drawn to that flame, incapable of looking away. It made you want to reach out and shelter it. Coax it into something brighter just to see how beautiful it could become. Even at the risk of being burned.

She wore a long white sundress. A color that nearly blended with her porcelain skin. It seemed to glow in the light of the monitor. *She* seemed to glow. Like an angel.

I was looking at a freaking angel.

She never lifted her gaze from the screen. Never looked around. Never made eye contact. I watched from the stacks as an older man settled at the machine beside her. Rather than acknowledge him, she curled deeper into herself as though she were trying to disappear. But invisibility was only something one could accomplish if others allowed it, and I wasn't ready to stop seeing her, yet.

She typed at a frantic pace, fingers flying over the keys, but I was too distracted by her eyes to really notice. Eyes that widened unbearably huge as a commotion broke out near the front desk. Raised voices penetrated the hushed atmosphere like a bullet through glass, shattering the silence.

I watched her jab repeatedly at the Print button, nerves making her movements uncoordinated and jerky. When the old laser jet whirred to life, she scooted back from the desk and hurried over to where a stack of papers was piling up. Her fear became my fear. I felt it deep in my gut and I had to know . . . What made this angel so afraid?

So I followed her.

"Where the hell is she?" A woman was leaning heavily against the desk, getting in the librarian's face. "Insisted I come pick her lazy ass up and now—"

"Mom. I'm here. I'm sorry, I—" The blue eyed girl came to a stop a solid three feet from her mother and seemed to realize that words weren't going to do her any good.

The woman looked ready to breathe fire. And she might have if there had been an open flame in the general vicinity. I could smell the alcohol on her breath from across the small lobby.

"Well, it's about damn time."

"I'm sorry. I didn't mean to miss the bus. I was—"

"Stop acting like a kicked puppy. You're such a damn good actress. Always getting exactly what you want, aren't you? What happened your highness, fall off that high horse of yours?"

"Mom, please, can we not do this here?" Anxious eyes bounced around the busy room, a fiery red blush creeping into her cheeks. "We can talk about it at home if—"

"Home? Is that where you want me to take you? Why, yes, Your Majesty. Please, allow me to chauffer you home."

The girl shrank under the weight of sarcasm, gnawing viciously at the lower lip trapped between her merciless teeth. Obviously not a stranger to this type of treatment, she seemed more concerned with the growing audience beginning to take notice than the abuse being hurled at her. She looked mortified. As though *she* had anything to be ashamed of.

I felt my muscles strain and my hands roll into tight fists at my sides.

"Is this what was so important you had to waste my time to come out here? *Stupid* papers for some *stupid* class you're too *stupid* to pass, anyway?" The woman reached for the stack of papers, but her aim was off. All she managed to do was knock them to the floor. With a frustrated kick that nearly landed her on her ass, she sent them fluttering across the carpet.

The girl scanned the scattered pages with dismay before bravely facing the irate woman behind the desk. "I'm sorry. I'm so sorry."

The librarian from hell looked about two seconds from calling the cops. I couldn't let that happen. That poor girl had enough to deal with already.

"Excuse me?"

A pair of angry eyes swung in my direction, intensified by the small glasses perched on her nose.

"Hi. Um . . . I was wondering if you could tell me where to find documentation on the effects of . . ." I was suddenly feeling inspired. "Addiction. On morality."

"Mom, *please*." The girl tugged on her mother's arm only to have it ripped away from her. "Can we just go?"

"Get your ass in the car. You can sit in the back. I can't stand to look at you. You make me sick." Abandoning all of her hard work, the girl's hair fell like a curtain, hiding those stunning eyes as she ducked her head and scurried toward the door, her mother staggering along behind her. "I should have just left you here. You're not worth the gas money I wasted coming to get your sorry ass."

The door fell shut behind them with a gust that sent several stray pages drifting across the floor, coming to rest at my feet. The sound of that terrible woman's voice dug into my brain as I crouched to gather them all up. Who said things like that? In public? To their own daughter? Acid churned my stomach as I stacked the papers on the desk in case she had a chance to come back for them, and I realized the whole scene had made me physically ill.

"I'm sorry. Do you have a bathroom?"

The librarian nodded stiffly toward a door across from the seating area. "Through there."

Several pairs of eyes that had abandoned their laptops, tablets, and phones long enough to take in some real world drama tracked my progress. Evidently, inserting myself in the situation had made me someone worthy of interest. That was the problem with the world—*one* of the problems. Everyone spent so much damn time staring at a screen—myself included—that when real life was happening right in front of them, they acted like it wasn't. Like other people weren't people, but performers in a show for their entertainment. Socialization, compassion, empathy . . . They were becoming nothing more than words.

Cool water felt good against my overheated skin. I was so angry it was making my blood boil.

. . . And frying my brain cells. *Shit!*

My reflection stared back at me in disbelief. I just watched that girl go with that woman—that *clearly intoxicated* woman—to get in a *car*. We all did.

The muffled bang of the bathroom door against the pale blue wall sounded obnoxiously loud in the renewed stillness of the library. Everyone had gone back to their gizmos and gadgets, going on with their lives without a second thought for Angel.

Damn them—and me—if anything should happen to her.

The librarian tried to signal me as I blew past her, pointing to a pile of books stacked on her desk. I didn't have time for that.

My car was parked in the second row, right where I'd left it, surrounded by nearly a dozen other vehicles. Everything from SUVs to motorcycles. But no Angel.

She was gone.

I'd found an *Angel*. And I'd let her get away.

Two

"He did *what*?" I shook my head at the phone in my hand as though it could somehow erase the words I'd just heard, like some kind of mental etch-a-sketch. It didn't work. A woman's irritated voice continued to babble down the line, affirming that I hadn't heard her wrong the first time around. "Yes. Thank you for calling. I'll be right there."

Slamming the house phone back into its cradle, I snapped off the pot of water just beginning to boil and scowled at the uncooked noodles on the counter.

When it came to school, I'd been on Kiernan's side from the start. All kids gripe about having to learn things they'll never use in their lives. For most, it was probably true. For Kiernan, it was an indisputable fact. Unless they were discovering the cure to cancer in high school chem lab, there was no point. Not for him.

But Mom insisted. Said he needed to get out of the house. Be more social. 'Act normal, feel normal' practically became the woman's mantra. And when she set her mind to something, there really was no stopping her.

But there was a fatal flaw in her logic. We *weren't* normal. Kiernan wasn't normal. And normal situations didn't affect him in a normal way.

Normally, it would be a parent going into the principal's office to collect him for his suspension. *Normally*, he'd be taken home, chewed out, and sent to his room or something. But, as I said, we weren't normal.

It wasn't anger or even disappointment that had me squeezing my keys tight enough that their tiny metal teeth bit into the palm of my hand in the hallway outside the office door. It was sickening dread.

When they first diagnosed Kiernan, they all talked at us using a lot of words, like gliomas, astrocytoma, and vascularization, which meant absolutely nothing to me. They used other words, too. Words like tumor, inoperable . . . and *terminal*. Words I understood the meaning of, but were still completely foreign in correlation with my family. My little brother.

At first, they gave Kiernan two to three months to live. *Three months*. That's 2,191 hours, 131,487 minutes, 7,889,238 seconds.

That's all. Period. The end.

Then, they started him on a bunch of treatments and medications that must have been doing their job, because three months rolled into four, and then six, and ten. He got to celebrate another birthday, another Thanksgiving, another Christmas with us. And, the next thing we knew, a year had gone by. A year of sitting on pins and needles just waiting for the day I got that call. The one that would change my life forever.

Grateful and terrified for every single one of those 31,536,000 seconds.

Today was not going to be that day. That's what I told myself as I stepped over the threshold. A plump woman with a poster reminding her to 'dance in the rain' was sitting behind a desk, sorting through a stack of papers.

"Hi. Um . . . I'm looking for Kiernan Parks?"

Her head snapped up and she frowned at me. An expression that wasn't nearly as intimidating as she probably would have liked it to be. Maybe it was the poster. Or the kitten figurines. Or the pencil she was using with the bright yellow suns all over it. But the woman couldn't pull off threatening if her life depended on it. I wondered how any of the students took her seriously.

"Your brother caused quite the scene in the lunchroom today."

"So I've heard." And yet, I still couldn't believe it. Getting into a fight with some jerk was more than just a right of teenaged male passage for my brother. It was dangerous. And he knew that. Kiernan wasn't stupid. "Where is he?"

She nodded off to my left and I twisted, coming to a dead stop when I spotted Kiernan slumped in a chair against the wall. I should have been pissed. Or, hell, if our lives were anything close to ordinary, I should have been amused. The thought of Mom losing it over something my perfect little brother did, instead of me for a change, should have made me giddy. Instead, I felt like I was going to be sick.

ANGEL

Dark, purple bruises shadowed his jaw, his lower lip was split and crusted with dry blood, and he held a plastic baggie packed with ice against his left eye.

I immediately retracted my earlier thought. He was a bleeding moron.

***

"What in the hell were you thinking?"

Kiernan barged down the deserted hallways and plowed through the front doors with enough force to rattle the glass in its metal frame.

"I'm talking to you!" My lips were moving. I could feel them. And I could hear the words coming out. But Kiernan's ears were firmly locked in the 'off' position.

He stormed across the visitor's lot and threw open my passenger side door, slamming it behind him hard enough to make me cringe. She may not have been as shiny and new as his, but a '67 Impala was a classic and she deserved to be treated with a little more respect than that.

"What is your problem?" I slid behind the wheel, but stopped short of putting the key in the ignition. We weren't going anywhere until I got some answers. "Kiernan."

15

"My *problem*? My problem is that they suspended me. They're sending me *home*." His teeth were grinding so hard it was a miracle he got the words out at all.

"For *fighting*." It felt like stating the obvious, but Kiernan's brain didn't seem to be firing on all cylinders today. "What did you expect to happen?"

"That's not the point." He sank deeper into his seat, arms folded across his chest with his phone wrapped up tight in a white knuckled grip.

"Chill out, okay?" Stress wasn't exactly good for him, either. "Take the day off. You know the suspension won't last long once Mom gets ahold of them."

"I don't care how long it lasts. I have to be there *now*."

"Why? What's so damn important about being at school today?"

"Nothing." He twisted to stare out the side window, effectively shutting me out. "Forget it."

"Fine." He wanted to stew in glorious teen angst, who was I to stop him? The car purred to life, warm vibrations stirring beneath me. "But you'd better come up with some better answers before Mom hears about this."

"She doesn't know?" Something ridiculously close to hope shone in my brother's eyes. As though she wouldn't be clued in with one look at his face.

"Not yet." Tires whirled smoothly over wet pavement. "Keep that ice on your face. Maybe you'll look pretty again by the time they let you back in."

Kiernan groaned when we parked in front of a four story, square brick building that looked like something any two-year-old with a bucket of Legos could build. His specialist's office—our first stop in making sure testosterone fueled stupidity was the biggest problem of the day. I couldn't blame him. If I'd been through half the things they'd put him through in the past year, I'd hate doctors, nurses, machines, medicines, and check-ups, too. But he'd brought this on himself. And it wasn't exactly the highlight of my day, either.

I found a seat in the corner of the lobby and flipped through the pages of one magazine after another. Pictures of old men walking their dogs and full page shots of purple pills weren't really doing it for me. Where was a *Sports Illustrated* when you needed one? Or maybe a *Playboy*?

Frustrated, I tossed my latest piece of gripping literature onto the growing pile beside me. Why did this have to take so damn long? It's not like I didn't have better things to do than sit around in that bland room with the hideous orange chairs. A bunch of sick, sad, miserable people waiting around with other sick, sad, miserable people for sick, sad, miserable news. Did a more depressing place on Earth exist?

If I'd brought my laptop at least I could have accomplished something. Or a nap certainly wouldn't hurt. My eyes burned with exhaustion, the consequence of staying up past three in the morning to finish a paper the day it was due. Something I seemed destined to be doing again tonight.

Stretching my legs out in front of me, I tried to rest my heavy head, but the chair back didn't even reach my shoulders. The smooth, narrow, rounded wood arm rests did nothing to support actual arm resting, either. If I ever got my hands on the idiot who designed that useless piece of furniture . . . Leaning forward, I planted elbows on knees, and dropped my head into my hands.

Not exactly the world's most comfortable position, but it would do.

"Hey, you ready?" Kiernan slapped my shoulder and an impressive string of vulgar profanities ran through my head. Why hadn't I shut my eyes twenty minutes earlier? Maybe we could have gotten out of there a little sooner.

"Yeah." Checking my pockets for phone and keys, I stretched my aching back and stood. "The doc going to call with the results? Let us know if the stupid sector of your brain is lighting up like a Christmas tree today?"

Kiernan waited until I was halfway through the door before letting it go. "He said it would probably take an hour or two."

Great. *More* waiting. "Why don't we go pick up your car and then hit the diner for lunch?"

"I already ate lunch." Kiernan strapped on his seatbelt and sat there, flipping his cellphone over and over in his hand.

"Well, I haven't." We were sitting in the same car, but Kiernan was a million miles away. "Hey, what's going on with you?"

"Nothing."

"Are you feeling okay?"

If looks could kill, the one Kiernan shot me would have resulted in a bloody mess. That was the number one taboo question with him. I knew that. And I understood it. But there were times when it needed to be asked. If for nothing more than my own peace of mind.

Of course, peace of mind only came with an answer. Something I did not get. Only the look of death and then he went right back to fiddling with his freaking phone.

"Got a call to make?"

"Yeah, actually, I do."

"Well, don't let me stop you."

Despite the fact that I was practically bilingual in sarcasm, Kiernan wasn't quite so fast at picking it up. "I don't have her number."

"*Kiernan!*"

"*What?*"

He could be so infuriating at times. "Would you just *talk* to me?"

"About what?"

"Gee, I don't know. Maybe the guy who pummeled your face?"

"You should see *his* face." There was a hint of pride in Kiernan's voice and I had to work hard to crush a grin.

"Kier—"

"He was giving her a hard time, alright? This assclown at school was giving his girlfriend—*ex*-girlfriend—a really hard time. Said some awful things. He hurt her, Cal."

A pair of frightened blue eyes came to mind. My nostrils flared and I felt my spine go rigid. Fighting over a girl was one thing, but fighting to defend one? How was I supposed to fault him for that? It was more than I'd done.

"She's a sweet girl. She's never hurt anyone. And all he does is put her down. He's the worst kind of bully and when she finally stood up to him . . ." Kiernan's face contorted, his eyes narrowing into slits and that vein that only bulged on his forehead when he was truly pissed popped out. "It's *my* fault. I convinced her to breakup with him. I told her I'd—"

"Kier, stop. It sounds like you did that girl a favor." One I wished I'd done for Angel.

"She's not going to see it that way." Kiernan's head dropped back against the seat. "I made her a promise. I promised her I'd be there. That she wouldn't have to face this alone. And now . . ."

"And now you're here. With me." His sudden epic love for education was starting make sense.

"I let him get to me and now I'm suspended. For who knows how long. And she's all alone. Exactly like I promised her she wouldn't be."

"I'll talk to Mom, tonight. We'll call the school. Everything will work out, okay? I'm sure she can make it through one day on her own."

Kiernan didn't seem quite as convinced, but he let the matter drop. There was nothing more either one of us could do about it.

"How about lunch? Or *second* lunch?"

"Sure." He frowned at his reflection in the blank screen of his phone and then shoved it in his pocket.

***

An hour later, I felt slightly nauseas watching Kiernan shovel food into his mouth. For someone who'd already eaten, he was certainly enjoying his burger and steak fries. The same could not be said for my turkey wrap. Normally, I could pack it away with the best of them, but I couldn't seem to find my appetite. Maybe it was the worms burrowing holes in the pit of my stomach.

Kiernan had this ability to turn things off that I envied. He could just not think about things. Or, at least, not worry about them. I guess when it comes down to shutting off your biggest fear or surrendering to it, you have to find a way. And once you can shut that out, the little things must become easy to ignore.

My phone felt like a lead weight in my pocket. It had started the meal on the table, but when I caught myself staring at it for the hundredth time, I'd put it away. Now I just imagined the blank screen staring back at me. Where was the doctor with those damn results?

"You gonna eat that?" Kiernan reached for my plate and I slid it across the swirl patterned table top to him.

A wrinkled old lady with friendly eyes and a warm smile, wearing a pale blue apron, bustled over to our table with a pot of coffee in hand. It would be my third cup, which would do nothing for my jittery nerves, but at least it would keep my eyes open.

"Anything else I can get you boys?" She topped off the mug and turned her smile on Kiernan, who could only manage to shake his head as he wiped a gob of mayo from his chin.

"No, thank you. We'll take the check." We'd killed as much time as possible. And if the doctor didn't call soon, I'd be killing him next.

"Sure thing, honey."

I'd been sitting on the edge of my seat for going on two hours, acutely aware of my phone. All of my thoughts centered on it. Maybe that's why when it started buzzing against my thigh, I nearly jumped out of my skin. I was in such a rush to free it that the stupid thing nearly ended up on the floor.

"Hello?"

"Caulder Parks? This is Doctor Fauler's office calling with test results for Kiernan . . ." I leaned forward, eyes glued to my brother, as she rattled off a battery of numbers.

As my brain processed the information, I saw the first true glimpse of fear from Kiernan. He really wasn't stupid.

When she finished up her spiel, followed by a long winded explanation of why fighting was a bad idea for my brother—as though I didn't already know—I thanked her and hung up.

"So? What did they say?"

I was tempted to withhold the information. Challenge him to own the fear I'd been battling since that first phone call came in from the school. And if it had been anything short of his *life* that we were talking about, I might have. "You're good. I mean, you're totally crappy. But no crappier than you were before."

The air of relief surrounding our table was palpable. It was like a giant balloon had been inflated around us, growing bigger and bigger, and finally . . . it burst. Pressure relieved, we could take a breath again. I sagged in my chair and eyed the full cup of coffee on the table in front of me.

Screw caffeine. I needed to sleep.

For a month.

Three

"Caulder? Hey, Parks, you still with us?"

I blinked at my notebook and the sunbaked blonde in front of me. "Hey. Yeah. Sorry, Beth. What did you say?"

"Are you alright?" Perfectly manicured nails wrapped around the back of my chair, and I caught a whiff of coconut as her hair fell over her shoulder and bushed against mine. "You sort of checked out for a minute or two."

More like the entire evening. *Shit*. What time was it? The rest of the class was busy packing up and I was still staring at a blank page.

"Yeah. Guess I've got other things on my mind."

"Obviously. Listen, I was going to go with Marjorie and Tom to get some pie. Do you wanna come? I could help you fill in some of those . . ." Beth glanced at my notebook and grimaced, "blanks."

"Pie?"

She shrugged. "Tom's got a thing for pie."

"Beth! Come on!" At the back of the lecture center, Marjorie, Beth's best friend, was waving dramatically toward the door.

She was a short girl, but she didn't seem it. Her personality was as fiery as the wild curls on her head. Everything about her was *loud*. Her voice, her hair, her clothes. In stark contrast to her counterpart, Tom was tall and lanky, and his color of choice seemed to be black. From his buzz cut to his boots . . . black. We'd been in class together for a few weeks and he'd attended a study group I was part of once, but I couldn't remember ever hearing him talk.

"So? You coming?" Beth waved at her friends and turned back to me.

I wasn't really in the market for friends. And if I was, I probably wouldn't have chosen the pair by the door. But Beth seemed like a nice girl. We'd talk a time or two over assignments and between classes. Plus, I'd just spaced out for a solid hour and a half. Maybe getting my mind off things wasn't such a bad idea. And I really needed those notes.

"Sure. Why not?"

"Great."

I followed Beth up the wide stairs between the stadium style seating and got the strangest look from Marjorie along the way. It was almost . . . giddy. They all piled into Tom's pickup, but I opted to drive myself. I had no idea where this place was that we were going, but I doubted I'd want to come all the way back to campus to pick up my car afterward.

I nearly choked when we pulled up to the entrance of the Golden Gates Country Club. Who the hell, north of the Mason Dixon, rolls up to a valet in a pickup truck? Even my baby barely lived up to the standards set by the Maseratis and Porsches making their exit as I climbed out from behind the wheel. I was wearing jeans and a hoodie, for chrissakes.

"Isn't there some kind of dress code or something?" I handed my keys off to the man in the purple vest and joined Beth near a podium.

"Don't worry about it." She shook her head. "Tom's parents own the place."

ANGEL

"Tom?" The guy in the torn black jeans, black tee, and black motorcycle boots? *His* parents owned a *country club*?

"Never guess, right?"

"You two lovebirds coming?" As Marjorie and Tom brushed past us, it was hard not to notice the way he was openly groping her ass.

Our sneakers squealed on dark, polished wood floors drawing foul looks from the men and women wearing sports jackets and heels, clustered in deep cream armchairs in a series of secluded seating areas. For eight o'clock on a weeknight, the place was unexpectedly crowded. It was standing room only around an intricately carved bar, displaying every type of top-shelf liquor known to mankind.

Thick burgundy area rugs and exotic plant life added to the affluent feel without being gaudy. Even I had to admit . . . "It's a nice place."

Tom glanced around, looking altogether unimpressed. "I hate this damn place."

Marjorie rolled her eyes and knocked his shoulder. "Then why'd you bring us here, silly?"

"They've got good pie."

There were several people seated in a posh waiting area. Marjorie sauntered past all of them. The hostess was busy making phone reservations, while Marjorie hovered over her, impatiently tapping her nails on the desk.

"Can I help you?" She deposited the phone and immediately turned her flustered attention to us.

"Yes. Party of four." Marjorie paused and when the woman started tapping at a tablet, she sighed loudly. "We're with *Thomas Arnold*."

"Oh." The receptionist's gaze swung toward us again, quickly scanning myself and Tom. "I'm so sorry. It's crazy here tonight. Let me see what's available." She tapped away for a few more seconds and breathed a relieved sigh. "Here we go. There's a table available, if you'll follow me."

We trailed her through a busy dining room to a formal table set with white linens and china plates. All for *pie*. The entire experience, so far, had been surreal. And it only got stranger from there.

Surrounded by men in fancy suits and women in fancy dresses, Tom in his black wardrobe and Marjorie in her hot pink skirt and lime green tee started making out. Right there at the table. And it wasn't an innocent kiss. No, there was definitely some tonsil licking going on.

"So . . ." Beth cleared her throat and drew my attention away from the beginnings of a porno going on across from us. "Have you decided on a paper topic for Graff's class, yet?"

The pre-med program was somewhat limited. And with large class sizes, it wasn't surprising that Beth and I had more than a few together.

"The effects of addiction." I didn't mention the particular angle I was focusing on because I really didn't want to talk about it.

I had a ton of information to work with. The books from the library turned out to be surprisingly helpful, and it was coming together pretty easily. Minus the twenty or so pencils I'd snapped in half, trying to take notes.

Alcohol and drugs affect the brain, making an addict forgetful and moody. They often times have trouble expressing that anger and tend to misdirect it toward those around them. Many lack empathy. All of which leads to an increased risk of abuse—both verbal and physical.

And that was just chapter one.

"Here you are." A waitress with a long brown braid stopped at our table and unloaded four plates of cherry pie we hadn't even ordered. Evidently, this kind of thing wasn't uncommon for Tom.

He and Marjorie didn't even bother to break their lip lock long enough to acknowledge the woman, so I thanked her and handed out the plates, leaving mine untouched in the middle.

"You don't want any?" Beth tipped her head to look up at me as she unwrapped her silverware and draped the napkin across her lap.

"Not really hungry. What about you? What are you writing about?"

A subtle flush crept up her neck. "This is going to sound totally girlie, but I'm writing my paper on love. Not *love* love. That's not just a human thing. I mean, I know penguins and wolves and whatever mate for life, and that could be considered love. I'm writing about the cultivation of love. Courtship." Her eyes darted across the table. "Making out in country clubs. That type of thing."

I stared at her long enough to watch her blush grow darker before letting her off the hook. "That's a cool idea. Penguins, huh?"

ANGEL

Popping a bite of pie in her mouth, Beth grinned around her fork. "And wolves."

"Fascinating."

"Not as fascinating as . . ." She swept her gaze over to where Tom looked about two seconds shy of pinning Marjorie to the booth. "Us."

True. Animals were fairly predictable. They operated off of survival instincts. They did what made sense. Humans? We pretty much did the opposite of that.

Beth glanced at the time on her phone and sighed. "I can't stay long. I have to swing by the library before it closes. I swear it feels like I live there these days. Seriously, I should just set up a tent in the lobby. A cot, reading lamp . . . I'd be good to go."

She wasn't the only one spending an inordinate amount of time at the library, recently. I'd been back to the local branch seven times in two weeks. For 'research purposes'. *She* hadn't been there. And I hadn't left with anything more than a deep sense of disappointment.

"You probably want to add some pie to that list." I eyeballed the remnants of cherry sauce and crust crumbs on her plate.

"It's delicious." She laughed, swiping a finger through some leftover red goo and lifting it to her lips. "You sure you don't want to try some?"

"Nah. I'm good." Sleep had become nearly impossible even without added late night sugar.

Angel haunted my dreams. Nightmares filled with angry voices and cruel words. Sad blue eyes, desperately seeking salvation. But I could never reach her. No matter how hard I tried, every time I came close, she was dragged away by pitiless hands.

I should have done something. Said something. I never should have let her leave that day.

"What class is this paper for?" *Hallelujah.* Tom had peeled himself off of Marjorie long enough to notice there were other people at the table.

"Social Sciences." Beth made a gagging sound and I couldn't disagree. It was one of the worst classes I'd taken.

"Right." Tom nodded as though he were making a mental note of the information. "Remind me never to take that class. Leave the paper writing to you smart people."

ANGEL

"You're smart, Tom," Marjorie scolded. "You're taking Intro to the Human Body with us."

"Only because *you* are."

"Aww." Marjorie swooned. As in, actually swooned. I'd always thought that was more of a word and not so much an actual physical occurrence, but there it was. Right before my eyes.

The two of them were back at it again before they'd even had time to catch their breath. Beside me, Beth giggled and shook her head.

"They can be a bit . . . much, sometimes."

"Ya think? I'm suddenly glad I passed on the pie."

I was only half joking, but Beth laughed anyway.

We tried to hold a somewhat normal conversation, while more and more eyes turned to our table. Most of them looked disgusted. More than ready to call it a night, I considered making my great escape, but I couldn't leave Beth there alone with the two of them.

"You want a lift to the library? It doesn't look like Tom's going to be ready to leave anytime soon."

"Yes." She nodded and reached for the jacket hanging from the back of her chair. "Please."

We didn't bother saying goodbye. They wouldn't have noticed if we had.

Outside, the temperature was beginning to drop and I groaned. It wasn't even October yet and I was already cold. Winter was going to suck.

"Thin blooded, huh?" Beth was grinning up at me.

"Like water. Pathetic, I know."

"I'd offer you my coat, but I don't think it'd fit." She looked very amused with herself.

"Ha-ha. Cute. Make fun of the guy freezing his ass off. Who also happens to be the guy giving you a lift."

Her only response was to smile wider.

"Your car, sir." A man in a purple vest passed off my keys and I thanked him with a generous tip for getting us out of there before frostbite set in.

When Beth was buckled into my passenger seat, I pulled out and headed back toward campus. So much for my quick escape. We drove in silence for a while—mostly, because I was concentrating on how to get back to campus without having to use my GPS: it's a guy thing— before Beth shifted so that her back was against the door and she was facing me.

"Thanks for the ride. It might have taken me a while to pry those two apart."

"And the Jaws of Life." I couldn't offer the same kind of undivided attention she was giving me, sparing only a glance in her direction. "No offense, Beth, but why do you hang out with them? They don't even talk to you."

She shrugged. "They're not always that bad. Tom just likes to rub it in his parent's faces. They don't like Marjorie very much."

I couldn't imagine why. "Uh huh."

We turned onto campus and I pulled up outside the library.

"Here." She pulled out a purple notebook and dropped it on my dash. "All the notes are dated. Copy whatever you need and you can just bring it back to me at study group."

"Thanks, Beth. You're a lifesaver."

"Thank *you*. For coming tonight. I didn't know he was taking us there, I swear, or I wouldn't have asked you."

"It's alright."

"Well, you saved me, so . . ." Beth leaned across the seat and before my brain could process what was happening, she'd planted a kiss on my cheek and was reaching for the door handle. "Thanks."

Four

I finished the assignment I had due by midnight for an online course I'd enrolled in to supplement my night classes and stretched my sore neck. Researching disease and mortality rates was a real bitch when your own brother was a living, breathing example. Sometimes pre-med studies hit just a little too close to home and I had to wonder if deep down I wasn't some kind of masochist.

There was more that needed to get done. There was always more. But a man needs to eat and the delicious scents wafting upstairs for the past hour let me know that dinner was probably already on the table.

Most nights we ate at the small table in the kitchen. With just the three of us, using the larger one in the dining room felt like a waste. Plus it was some fancy kind of wood Mom picked out and polishing it was a real pain in the ass. Not tonight, though. Tonight I heard voices coming from the dining room as I hit the bottom of the stairs.

Predominantly, Mom's. "Caulder is quite the rebel. Thinks he's proving something by being late to every meal. All he really gets is cold food."

Rolling my eyes, I crossed the kitchen, following my nose at the demands of my stomach.

"I'm not rebelling, Mom. I'm just—" I took one look at the table and froze. I couldn't believe my eyes. It was *her*. The girl who had been consuming my every thought for weeks. Sitting at my dinner table. Beside my brother. "I'm just busy."

"Busy-schmusy. We have company."

"So I see." Taking a seat beside Mom, I pinched my arm beneath the table, convinced I'd fallen asleep doing homework and this was some sort of elaborate dream. It wasn't. "And who is this?"

"Oh, I'm sorry." Kiernan's hand brushed over her shoulder as he made the introductions. "This is Jade. Jade, my brother Caulder."

ANGEL

Jade. The angel had a name.

"Nice to meet you." Jade's voice was as small as the rest of her.

I wanted to answer her, talk to her, *acknowledge* her, but my brain was too busy running in overdrive, working through what I was seeing. It was clear from the way she subtly leaned into him, the way she looked to him for guidance . . . This wasn't some friend he'd picked up at school. She wasn't a lab partner over to work on a class project. Kiernan meant something to this girl. Meant a *lot* to her.

And she had absolutely no clue what she was getting herself into.

"You invited her over for a family dinner?" What kind of game was he playing?

"Yeah. I did." Kiernan shot me a look that dared me to ask the question on the tip of my tongue.

So, I did. "So, what? Are you two . . . dating?"

"Cal!" Mom was pissed, but that was something I'd have to deal with later. I had bigger concerns at the moment.

How well did Kiernan even know her? Did he have any idea what kind of crap she already had going on in her life? That he was only going to make it worse? It wasn't something we'd ever talked about, but I'd always assumed that when the Kiernan bomb imminently exploded, it would only be Mom and me blown to pieces by the blast. Collateral damage was never a part of the plan.

"That's really none of your damn business." Kiernan bunched his napkin in his fist and glanced at Jade.

I got the impression that neither of them knew the answer to that question. He was playing fast and loose with not only his emotions, but hers. And it was only going to end one way. *Badly*.

"No. You're right, it's none of my business. But don't you think it's hers?"

The blood drained from Kiernan's face and I had the answer to at least one of my questions. He knew what he was doing to her. He knew it wasn't right. And yet, there she was, sitting right beside him, looking lost and confused.

"Maybe I should just—" She started to push away from the table, but Kiernan was quick to stop her.

"No. You're not leaving."

ANGEL

Of course she wasn't. Because letting her go would have been the decent thing to do. "By all means, you stay. I'm not hungry anyway."

Shooting a look at my little brother that promised we'd be having words about this later, I excused myself from the room. I couldn't look at her, anymore. I couldn't watch those shadowed eyes, permanently ingrained in my memory, look at my brother with a trust he didn't deserve. I couldn't be a witness to the charade he was putting on. And I sure as hell wouldn't be a part of it.

I'd reached the top of the stairs before I remembered to breathe. Dammit, I was no good with change. And there had been far too much of it in our lives recently. None of it good. And now . . . The *literal* girl of my dreams shows up at my house. *With my brother.*

Anger seemed to cook inside of me at a constant simmer, but at times like these—when I was stressed and unprepared—it would boil over. It wasn't that Kiernan hadn't deserved it, but he hadn't been the only one on the receiving end. I'd officially known Angel—*Jade*—for all of five minutes and she probably already hated my guts.

Kiernan and I weren't done. Not by a long shot. We were going to have a very serious discussion about this. Very soon. But for now, I put that aside and headed back downstairs to apologize to our guest. Only she wasn't in the dining room, anymore. She was standing frozen in the hallway, eyes riveted to the closed door of Mom's home office.

"He can't treat Jade that way. She doesn't understand." Kiernan's voice filtered easily into the hall.

"I get that, Kiernan. I think that's half the problem, though."

"No, you don't get it, Mom. She gets that shit from everyone else in her life. Kids at school, that asshole ex-boyfriend of hers, even her own mother, for chrissakes." A tiny gasp left Jade at Kiernan's mention of her mother, and her entire body locked up tighter than before. "You should hear the crap that woman heaps on her. Always telling her she's not good enough. Making her feel unworthy. Unloved. Like she's some kind of burden. And she believes it. Every damn word. She can't see any of the good in herself because no one shows her. I am *trying*. I'm trying to make her see, but then Cal comes in and says stuff like that. There's no way she'll believe it's not about her. Doesn't matter what I say now. She is convinced she's not good enough for anyone. And now Caulder's gone and—"

What had I done? Jade's gaze continued to bore into the door unaware of mine boring into her. Looking beneath the surface, trying to piece together what Kiernan was saying with all of that emotion in her eyes. The picture was blurry, but I was getting the distinct impression that it wasn't pretty. And that I'd only managed to make it uglier.

"He didn't know, Kiernan. This is not entirely his fault. You know he's just—"

"*I* know, but *she* doesn't."

My mind ran back over the things it hadn't had the chance to process before they'd come spewing out of my big mouth earlier. Mom was wrong, I *did* know. But Kiernan was right, she didn't. She didn't have any clue what I was talking about. What must I have sounded like to her?

An outstanding asshole, that's what.

When she spun around with tears in her eyes, I could have choked on my guilt. "Jade, I— I'm sorry. I—"

"Oh, God." She looked like she was going to be sick. "Don't."

She broke into a jog, blowing past me before I could stop her. "*Wait!*"

I watched her fly around the corner and, a moment later, the sounds of the storm intensified before the front door slammed shut. Kiernan was still going at it with Mom, but she shouldn't be out there alone and I was probably the last person she ever wanted to see again.

Pausing long enough to rap once on the door, I threw it open to find Mom standing beside her desk, hands on her hips. A pose Kiernan and I both knew better than to mess with. *Usually.* Kiernan stood across from her, glaring daggers at me that were somehow less intimidating.

"She heard you." I stopped in the doorway and folded my arms. If this was a battleground, I wasn't going in with my defenses down.

"What?" Kiernan's eyes flicked past me into the empty hallway.

"Jade heard everything you said."

"Shit." He moved toward the door, knocking me out of his way. Something that only worked because I allowed it to. "Where is she?"

"She took off."

"In this weather?" Mom's 'resistance is futile' expression morphed into worry as her eyes tracked to the window where rain pelted up against the glass.

"Someone should go after her." My gaze flicked to Kiernan and he didn't need to be told twice.

Mom called after him to wear a jacket as he took off down the hallway. I was willing to bet that getting wet was the least of his worries.

When I heard the door slam for a second time, I returned my attention to Mom. Her hands were back on her hips. *Great*.

"Caulder Matthew, you were entirely out of line tonight."

"I know." It wasn't worth arguing. She was right.

"But I understand why you did it." Mom sank wearily into the chair behind her desk and I took the one on the opposite side.

"He's going to hurt her."

"I know."

"It isn't fair."

"I know."

"He *has* to tell her."

"I know." I sensed her 'but' coming before it ever left her lips. "But he's happy, Cal. I haven't seen Kiernan this passionate in a long time. About anything. And it's because of her."

I dropped my head into my hands and scrubbed at my face. I couldn't erase that look in Jade's eyes before she ran out. The utter devastation. It felt like a preview of things to come. I understood where Mom was coming from. She wanted her son to be happy. I wanted that, too. He was my brother, for crying out loud. Of course I wanted him to be happy. But, then, why did I feel so conflicted?

Was it wrong to want to spare the girl with the haunted eyes one more ghost?

Was it wrong to want whatever time Kiernan had left to be filled with as much happiness as possible?

Was there any *right* answer?

ANGEL

***

I scanned over the final three pages of my chemistry notes and tucked them away in a folder when I heard Kiernan's car in the drive. There was a test tonight and the last of my study time was about to be spent debating moral ethics. Taking a breath, I counted to ten and braced myself for impact.

"What the hell is wrong with you?" He burst into the room soaking wet.

"Don't bother knocking." Leaning back in the rolling chair, I planted both feet firmly on the carpeted floor. This needed to happen, whether or not I was ready for it.

"This isn't some kind of joke, you dickhead."

"*I'm* the dickhead? *Me*?" The chair banged off the desk as I lifted myself with more force than strictly necessary. "Do you have any idea how selfish you're being? The way she looks at you . . . To let her get attached like that just to—"

"Leave her? Yeah. The thought's crossed my mind a time or two."

He was right. I was a dickhead. The downside of arguing with your terminally ill little brother was that no matter what—right or wrong—you were *always* the dickhead.

"Don't do this, Kiernan." Yelling at him would get me nowhere, but I was willing to plead on her behalf. "You *know* it's not fair."

"I didn't *mean* to do this. I never meant to get close enough to hurt her. Christ, Cal, I think I love her. The *last* thing I want to do is hurt her."

Love her? He *loved* her?

"I was trying to be her *friend*."

"Yeah, well, you failed." My words had lost their bite. I slammed head first into that concrete wall of resignation and slumped back into my chair. "You know this is a clusterfuck just waiting to happen, right?"

"I know." Kiernan sank onto my bed and buried his face in his hands. "What am I supposed to do? I've screwed this all up." His eyes lifted to me, silently pleading for a solution I didn't have.

My fingers moved in idle circles, massaging my temples. I could feel a headache coming on. "One look at her and you can see that she's falling for you, too. But, Kier . . . She only knows *half* the person she's opening her heart to. And she doesn't strike me as the type to open it easily. You can't do that to her. There's a point where secrets become lies. Kiernan . . ." I felt like I was walking a verbal tightrope, teetering over the right words to make my point. "Your condition doesn't define you. It's not who you are. Jade knows who you are. And she seems to like it for some reason." Kiernan huffed a minute laugh and I felt the burn of tears begin to rise. Swallowing hard, I forced my voice to remain even. "It is a factor, though. I wish it wasn't, but it is. You can't just pretend it doesn't exist. And you can't keep it from her. She has a right to know—" The lump in my throat threatened to cut off my oxygen supply and my voice broke into a croak.

"That she's falling for a ticking time bomb?"

"Kiernan . . ."

"I know. I know she does. I know I have to tell her. I just don't know how to do it." He poked at the growing dark spot forming around his sopping jeans on my bedspread, but made no move to get off of it. "Everyone hurts her, Cal. *Everyone.* Even people who aren't trying to." The 'like you' was silent, but I heard it anyway. "I just don't want to add my name to that list."

"Kiernan." I rubbed my eyes followed by the back of my neck. I felt sore and tense everywhere. "I'm your brother. I love you. I don't want to hurt you the way you don't want to hurt her, but I'm going to be brutally honest with you. The way you need to be with Jade. You are going to hurt her. There's no getting around that. When you care about someone . . ." I took a deep breath. I'd promised him brutal honesty and that's what I'd give him. "When you care about someone you're going to lose, it hurts. But that's not *your* fault. You're not hurting her on purpose by telling her. You're not even hurting her by accident. You didn't *choose* this. You care about her? You love her? You don't *want* to leave her. The only way you're hurting her is by *not* telling her." At this point, I figured we'd both reached our 'touchy-feely' quota for the day. I was brain fried from recent events and the cracks in my façade were beginning to show. If I couldn't lighten the mood, the whole thing was likely to come crumbling down. Plastering on a grin that felt no more real than the smiley face sticker Kiernan had stuck to the bottom of my desk when we were kids, I slugged him on the shoulder. "So, grow a pair and tell her already. And while you're at it, tell her how you feel about her, you chickenshit."

ANGEL

Kiernan's answering smile was no more convincing than that damn sticker.

Five

"Cal! Wake up!"

"What?" My eyes sprung open and clocked the darkness still filling the room in about as much time as it took the rest of me to bolt upright in bed. "What is it? What's wrong?"

Kiernan stood beside my desk, hair disheveled from sleep, but fully dressed in jeans and a hoodie. "Nothing. Relax."

"Relax?" Jesus Christ, my heart felt like a battering ram trying to bust through my ribcage. "You just barged into my room in the middle of the night like the house is on fire and you're telling me to *relax*?"

"It's not about me, okay? But I need your help."

"Help with what?" I don't even know why I bothered to ask. I was already half out of bed, knowing full-well that whatever the answer was, I'd do it.

"Jade. She's in trouble."

I froze with only one pant leg on. It had been over a week since my not-so-smooth introduction to the girl. Kiernan barely spoke about her and I didn't ask. If I did, I was pretty sure I knew what the answer would be, and then I'd have to say something. I didn't want to say something. Kiernan was happy. As long as I didn't think about whose expense that happiness came at, I could be happy for him.

"What kind of trouble?" Jade struck me as the quiet type. I couldn't imagine her getting into the kind of trouble that required a two A.M. wake up call. I also couldn't imagine, of all the people on the planet, she'd want *my* help. But if she was desperate enough that Kiernan was there asking for it, she was going to get it. Like it or not.

"The kind that involves the police. Hurry up." He waved impatiently at my half-dressed body.

Stumbling around, I managed to pull my other leg through the jeans and slip a long sleeved thermal over my head. "She got arrested?"

"Not yet. Let's go before she does."

***

The farther we drove the tighter the knot in my stomach grew. We sped through the nicer part of town where we were fortunate enough to live, past the somewhat underdeveloped area, and deep into the downright scary section.

"What the hell was she thinking coming out here alone at night?" My stomach turned over at the thought of what could have happened to her.

"I don't know." Kiernan slowed to check a street sign and then pressed on the gas. "She was supposed deliver something."

"What?"

"I didn't waste time with the details, Cal. All I know is the police are there and whatever it is, she doesn't want them finding it."

Made sense considering where we were. And *when*. Somehow I doubted UPS was still on the clock. But I was having trouble picturing Jade as being the kind of person to transport legally questionable substances to sanity questionable locations.

ANGEL

"Where did she say she was?" Better to get to her, first, and figure the rest out, later.

"Corner of Seventh and Main." Kiernan slowed to a roll and I peered through the darkness at a sign for Sixth Street.

"One more block. Go."

We rolled down the rutted street fast enough not to draw attention, scoping out the sketchy landscape for any sign of her.

"There." She stood, half hidden in shadow on a dark, damp street corner. As out of place as the sun at midnight.

She wasn't dumb enough not to know how much danger she'd put herself in by being there. That much was clear from the terror illuminated in her face by the flashing red and blue lights. Just reckless enough to be there, anyway.

I watched Kiernan wrestle a box from her and toss it in the backseat. Two cop cars sat parked outside a decaying house across the road. Her intended destination, I assumed. God help her if she'd actually gone inside that place.

Jade slid in next, making a noticeable effort to distance herself from the package, as though it may grow fangs and bite her. Followed by

Kiernan. We didn't waste time on words. He pulled a uey—an illegal maneuver that probably wasn't the best idea at the moment—and got the hell out of Dodge.

The speedometer barely ticked the speed limit as we coasted down silent, deserted streets. I watched Jade wringing her fingers in the visor mirror as we drove. Straight, white teeth gnawed frantically at her soft pink lower lip until the skin around it started to turn red. My fingers itched to reach out and rescue it, but I fisted them in my pant leg, instead.

It wasn't until we were in somewhat safer territory that Kiernan finally broke the pressurized silence. "Where are we headed?"

"I don't know." Panic rolled off of her, crashing around the car like a tidal wave of fear and anxiety. "I don't know what to do. DJ said if I screwed this up, he'd make me pay. But I can't deliver it. And I can't get rid of it. And I can't—"

"Rewind. Who's DJ?" Kiernan threw the car in park at a red light and twisted around to face her.

I was glad to hear he was as confused as I was.

ANGEL

"The guy I was delivering the box for. He lives in my complex. He doesn't have a super great reputation."

"So we've gathered." It was obvious she was scared spitless of the guy. What I really wanted to know was how the hell she got mixed up with him in the first place. I was guessing it had to do with more than making a little extra cash on the side.

"I owed him a favor. He called it in tonight. But I can't do what he asked and I don't know what to do about it. Or with that." Her voice shook almost as badly as the rest of her.

No doubt about it, she was in over her head. I didn't know a whole lot about drug dealers. It's not like they were a common occurrence in my life. But I did know one thing . . . As long as she had that box, Jade was in danger.

We couldn't get it where it needed to go, so that left only one other option. "Simple. We give it back."

***

The scrawling graffiti was a bold design choice for building management. One I could have lived without. It stretched down the hall in not-so-subtle shades of red, black, and an

59

interesting choice of lime green. Images that must have looked like something to somebody and words that weren't all spelled correctly. Whether that was intentional, or a reflection of the artist's lack of skill in other areas, I didn't know. And I didn't care. All I cared about was that *this* was where Jade lived. This was her *home*. She didn't even seem to notice the vandalism surrounding us. All of her attention focused solely on the wooden door with the number 3 hanging on front, where we'd come to a stop halfway down the first floor corridor.

My first guess: someone named DJ lived on the other side.

My second guess: I wasn't going to like him.

"Go ahead." I gave Jade a nudge forward when it became apparent she wasn't going to be able to do it herself.

She tapped lightly on the wooden surface and stepped back to wait. I wasn't quite as patient. My fist balled to pound on it when the door cracked open and a greasy head popped out. One look at Jade and the door swung wide. The guy standing there looked pretty much exactly the way I imagined he would. It was almost comical how cliché he was in his leather jacket and slicked back hair. He looked like he'd stepped right out of a bad sitcom.

Except the way he was staring at Jade. There was nothing funny about that.

"What the hell are you doing here? And who the hell are they?"

"Friends." I had to give the girl credit. She was shaking in her boots, but you'd never know it from the way she stood her ground and laid out what she'd come to say. "Listen, DJ, I did what you asked. I tried to deliver the package, but when I got there, the place was crawling with cops. I couldn't just walk in there. So I brought it back to you."

"You brought it back. And you brought them with you?" DJ cast a dismissive glance in our direction before returning to Jade.

I felt Kiernan shift beside me and I knew exactly what he was doing. Trying to draw attention away from Jade. *C'mon, asshole, look at us. Not her.*

It didn't work. Classic bully style, he focused on the weakest prey.

I'm not some chauvinistic jackass. The fact was, of the three of us, Jade *was* the weakest. Which made her his target.

"You fucked up, Jade. You fucked up, royally. You know what those people are going to do, they don't get the shit they bought? You know who's going to pay for that?"

I had an answer for him—one he wasn't going to like—but I kept my lips sealed. This was Jade's fight. He was *her* bully and if *she* was the one to stand up to him, it might actually make a difference. So, I was willing to let her handle things on her own.

Until the bastard made a move for her. Then all bets were off.

"Hey!" I wedged myself between them as Kiernan tugged Jade out of harm's way. *Bad move, jerk-off.* Now he had me to deal with. "The girl did what you asked. It's not her fault it went to hell. You're done now. You and her? It's done. Over. You don't talk to her again. You don't even look at her. You do and I swear, they'll have to mop up what's left of you. We clear?"

There wasn't a whole lot more I could have said to make myself any clearer. But when he craned his neck to look past me—at Jade—I knew he was as dumb as he looked.

My third guess: DJ was the one responsible for the masterpiece in the hallway.

"You live in my world, Jade. You can tell yourself different all you want with your books, and your studying, and your *'friends'*, but you're a sewer rat just like the rest of us." I heard her breath hitch behind me and it triggered every last one of my protective instincts. I clenched my fists to keep from doing something stupid, like pulling her into my arms and refusing to let her go. Focusing on the waste of human space in front of me, I funneled it into something much more familiar. Rage. And I had plenty. I may not have been able to take on Kiernan's demons, but Jade's I would gladly pummel into the ground. "And sewer rats stick together. They might be here to protect you now, but sooner or later, you're going to need my help again. It's only a matter of time. And when you do . . . the favor I have in mind . . . it's a little bit different."

His twisted grin made me physically ill. Evidently, DJ was more of a 'hands-on' learner.

"Son of a—" I was done talking. It was time to teach him a lesson he'd never forget.

Kiernan took his cue, herding Jade away from the scene as I laid into the dirtbag with every ounce of pent up fury I had in me. I hit him and I hit him. Again and again until the blood from my knuckles mingled with that from his busted face. He hit the floor hard and, God help me, there was a big part of me that wanted to keep going. To beat him into blood and bone. Release all of my anger. Give it somewhere to go, rather than let it continue to build inside of me. And make certain he never so much as looked in Jade's direction ever again.

Forcing myself to walk away was not easy. Hands still fisted tight enough that my raw knuckles stung, I stormed through the front door to where Kiernan stood, Jade tucked away in his arms.

"No more favors." If I couldn't do what I wanted to do to make sure he stayed away from her, the least I could do was make damn sure she never went near him, willingly, again.

"Enough, man." Kiernan shifted slightly, putting himself between her and me, as though I were the threat. "She's shaking like a leaf."

The red—which was all I was seeing—faded away and I saw that he wasn't lying. She was terrified, still suffering the aftershock of everything that had happened.

I choked back my frustration, locking it away where it belonged. She didn't deserve it. Not on top of everything else she'd been through. "How did you end up in this mess, anyway?"

"I—I owed him. He did me a favor."

"What kind of favor?" Kiernan tightened his arms around her, steadying her as she stumbled against his chest.

"I had to pick my mom up at a bar. She passed out on the ride home and it was too cold to leave her in the car all night. I didn't have enough gas to run the heater that long. So I asked DJ to help me get her upstairs."

"Let me get this straight." It hadn't taken a whole lot of imagination to assume I wasn't going to like this story, but this . . . It took every last ounce of self-control I possessed not to turn around and go back inside. And then find her mother's apartment and finish the job. "You had to go out alone, at night, to get your drunk mother and drag her ass back here. And then that bastard had the nerve to demand a favor in return for helping you get her inside?"

"Pretty much."

I was about two degrees short of that boiling point. Some small part of me had hoped the scene I'd witnessed in the library was a one-time ordeal, even knowing what Kiernan had said about her mother. There was no more fooling myself. "Like I said, no more favors."

Jade's face crumpled and I cursed my serious lack of brain-to-mouth filter around her. It should have been working overtime. Instead, it shut off completely. Luckily, my ever observant little brother stepped in to rescue us both from my loose lips.

"Jade, what he means is, if you ever need help, call me. Anything. Anytime. You call *me*, okay?"

"Or me. If Kiernan can't make it . . ." My chest pinched, knowing the only reason why that would be. And again, knowing she *didn't* know. "For any reason, you call me. Kiernan will give you my number. One of us will always be around."

Kiernan peered at me over Jade's head and, though silent, his gratitude was loud and clear.

Jade lifted her head from Kiernan's chest and sniffled back her tears as she swiped her damp cheeks against his shirt front. "Thank you. Both of you."

Her words were so sincere that they made me ache. She looked at not only Kiernan, but *me* with . . . awe? As though she couldn't believe we were there. Helping her. As though no one ever had before. And a sickened part of me was afraid that was exactly right.

"I mean it." Kiernan pressed a chaste kiss to her forehead, and I couldn't stand there any longer.

Even watching them from inside the car, I could feel that sickness growing. I told myself it was because he was still lying to her. I told myself it was because she still needed to learn the truth and face the pain that came with knowing it. I told myself it was out of fear for *them*. That's what I told myself.

Kiernan stood on the sidewalk, watching as Jade crossed the lot and disappeared inside another building with his hands shoved deep in his pockets to keep from reaching out and pulling her back. I knew this because my hands were shoved in my pockets, too.

Neither of us spoke as he slid behind the wheel and backed from the spot. Bathed in the unforgiving glare of our headlights, the crumbling foundation of the brick building looked even worse.

I stared out the side window, taking in as much depressing detail as I could from the poorly lit grounds of the dump Jade lived in. "It's bad, isn't it? Her situation. Worse than I thought."

"Yeah." Kiernan's made a right out of the complex and slumped, exhausted, back into his seat. "It's worse."

What a mess. I knew her mother was a grade-A bitch, but this girl had it coming at her from every angle. Her mom, her neighbor, some ex-boyfriend issues at school I didn't know much about, other than it was enough to get Kiernan into a fight. Something he'd never done before.

No wonder she was as timid as a field mouse half the time. Always hiding and shaking. The people who were supposed to protect her were the ones doing her the most harm. But she had a backbone in there somewhere. I'd caught a glimpse of it tonight. Everyone did. It was how we protected ourselves. But hers was buried so deep, I wondered if she even knew it was there. She reminded me, oddly, of a declawed cat.

ANGEL

Deprived of her ability to defend herself and tossed out into the wild.

"Dammit."

Kiernan flicked a glance in my direction. "Yeah."

I felt the pressure growing in my chest. The vice-like tightness, threatening to crush my rib cage. *Not now. Not here. Not like this.* I'd been hiding my panic attacks from everyone for over a year. I sure as hell wasn't about to have one in Kiernan's car.

Anchoring my hand in the hair at the back of my head, pulling hard enough at the roots to ground me in the present, I bent my neck and stared at the floor boards, forcing a few deep breaths into my lungs. "What are we gonna do?"

"What *can* we do? She's seventeen. It's not like we can kidnap her." Kiernan kept his tone casual, but the glow from the dashboard gave away the white knuckled grip with which he was strangling the wheel.

There had to be something I could do. For Jade. For Kiernan. For everyone. There were people in my life who needed me, counted on me. The number was only growing and I was failing them. All of them. Just as useless to help the new as the old. What good was I if I couldn't protect the people that mattered most to me and my family?

"We'll find a way. There has to be something we can—"

"We can't get her out of there. Trust me, I've looked into it. Any legal avenues would take . . . Might as well just wait for her birthday. Besides, she wouldn't leave. Her mother's heaped on the guilt so heavily, it's trapped her there. She's buried alive, Cal. The best we can do is help her find a way to survive it."

That wasn't good enough. I didn't want to help her weather the blows. I wanted to shield her from them. I knew my brother. He wanted the same. And yet there was one blow he could offer her some protection from, but he refused.

"You want her to survive? Then you *have* to tell her the truth. I get that you're afraid. I get that you have a lot to lose. But you want to do something for her? You want to protect her? *That* is where you start."

Most of Kiernan's face was concealed in shadow, but in the silence of the car I could hear the acceleration in his breathing. "I know. I will."

ANGEL

The same answer I'd been getting for weeks. I wanted to push it, remind him how unfair he was being. The longer he waited the worse it would be. But it had been a long night and we were both exhausted. She'd find out one way or another, soon enough. I just hoped it was the *right* way.

Six

"No. Chapter *seven*."

Tom slapped his textbook shut and glared across the oversized, round table at Alex, the fifth and final member of our study group. "He said chapter *six* was going to be on the test."

We'd been meeting together every Wednesday night since the beginning of the semester and it occurred to me that I didn't know a single one of their last names. Or anything about them outside of the fact that they were studying Intro to the Human Body. *Pathetic.* Other than Beth, I didn't even know what they were majoring in. The classic college icebreaker question and I hadn't even bothered to ask it.

ANGEL

"Guys." Beth sighed and rubbed at her forehead. "Did we cover chapters *six and seven* in class? Then they're *both* going to be on the midterm. We can't concentrate on just one chapter. We have to review them all or we're never going to pass."

She wasn't wrong. This exam was going to be a nightmare. I wouldn't have been surprised if the professor asked his middle friggin' initial. He wouldn't even give us a study guide. Apparently, if we'd been paying attention in class, we shouldn't need one. Well, I'd been paying attention—mostly—and let me tell you, I *needed* one. Fourteen chapters on the anatomy and functions of the human body were not something the human brain naturally stored, I knew that much for sure.

"Why don't we just start at the beginning and work our way through?"

No one was pleased with my suggestion, Marjorie groaning out loud. Beth was the only one who seemed to get that not *wanting* to do it and not *having* to do it were two entirely different things. She flipped to the front of her book and opened it to page one.

Only four-hundred-and-seventy-six more to go.

***

Ulna, radius, collarbone . . . My pencil drifted over the lined paper, giving shape to the source of all my troubles: the human body. Trachea, epiglottis, mandible, maxilla. Long, thin nasal bone. High zygomatic arches. Orbital eye sockets filled with eyes so blue they—

I jerked my hand away from the image, leaving a long gray streak, and stared at the page. My mockup of the human skeleton had taken on a life of its own. Fleshed into a person . . . A girl.

Jade stared back at me from my notebook. She was in black and white, but I could see the color of her eyes, her hair, her pale pink lips. Right down to the tiny dent in her nose.

"Shit." Slapping the book closed on her image, I shoved it in my laptop case.

Beth glanced up from her own notes. "Everything alright?"

"Yeah. I . . . uh . . . I just realized there's somewhere else I need to be." Throwing the case over my shoulder, I headed for the door as quickly as my legs could carry me.

ANGEL

This wasn't working. My mind was in so many different places, I couldn't concentrate on any of them. Even engulfed in the calming silence of the campus library, surrounded by people doing nothing but studying the same boring crap as me, I still couldn't focus.

My brain felt like one of those mirrored funhouses. Every time I turned around I saw something else. Sometimes the images mixed and warped together, but none of them ever came through clearly. I was losing my damn mind.

"Somewhere else? Caulder . . ." Beth left her books and papers behind to scurry after me, bringing me to a stop just inside the doors. "You know this test makes up half of our grade, right?"

"Yeah." When I wasn't dealing with doctors, and nurses, and *drug dealers*, it was absolutely my first priority. "I know."

Beth was a smart girl. She worked hard and studied harder. It made sense that she'd have trouble understanding that anything else could come first. Besides my particular set of circumstances, I really couldn't think of much else. Unfortunately, my circumstances were my circumstances, and that was life.

"Alright, well, we're squeezing in one last study session tomorrow night. Maybe we could grab coffee, beforehand? Pull an all-nighter?"

"I don't know." I scrubbed at my face, trying to find a blank slate to work from. "Maybe."

"Maybe? Caulder, this is serious."

I knew it was serious. Everything, my whole damn life, was serious.

"I *know* that!" The intern behind the desk hushed me and I dropped my voice. "Sorry. I know. I'm just . . . tired. I can't concentrate. I'll call you tomorrow, okay?"

"Sure." She tossed her hair over her shoulder and nodded. "Get some sleep. We'll try again tomorrow."

Try again tomorrow. The theme of my life. Every morning I'd wake up thinking, 'time to try again'. And every night I'd go to bed, telling myself, 'maybe tomorrow'.

ANGEL

Seven

Phones were a necessary evil in our lives. Necessary in case of emergencies. Evil for pretty much the same reason. Every damn time that phone rang my heart seized. A year and a half of mini-strokes at the sound of the bell. I learned really quick not to use a song I liked for a ringtone. I still couldn't listen to Maroon 5 without feeling residual tightness in my chest.

So when I answered it the following afternoon and Mom was in tears, I had to grab ahold of the counter for support.

"What happened?" I wasn't quite able to get a grip on the slight quiver in my voice, but it was concealed by Mom's sniffling as she tried to get control of herself long enough to communicate in something resembling a human language.

By the time I had the story, or most of it, I was already in my car. The hospital was the preset destination in mind and one of the reasons we chose the house we did. It wasn't far away. A quick shot on the highway and I could be there in less than ten minutes.

If I sped. A little.

Or a lot.

A seizure. It wasn't the first time I'd gotten that call. Kiernan had suffered seizures twice before, both minor. As minor as a *seizure* could be, anyway. But this time was different. This time Jade was involved.

Thumping the steering wheel with impatience, I nearly missed the ambulance passing me on the right as I sat in the turning lane. It swerved around me, cutting a gap in traffic with its flashing lights and blaring sirens to pull into the Emergency lot. Using the momentary pause in the endless stream of cars to my advantage, I swerved in behind it and pulled into the first available parking space I laid eyes on. Not giving a damn if it was handicapped or anything else.

A blast of air washed over me as I stepped through the sliding glass doors. Mom was hard to miss, giving hell to the poor woman in pale blue scrubs behind the admissions desk. I almost felt bad for her. Mom was a good person—the *best*—but when it came to her kids . . . You really didn't want to stand in her way.

I was on my way over to try to tame the beast when the doors on the opposite side of the room whooshed open and Jade shuffled through. She looked like she was in some kind of trance. Blank face, scanning the room with glazed eyes until they settled on Mom. She took one step and then another on shaky legs.

I don't remember telling my feet to move, but somehow I was right there, catching her in my arms when they gave out.

"Whoa there. You alright?"

It wasn't just her legs that were shaking. Her entire body trembled against mine and she was as white as a sheet. If I had to guess, I'd say she was bordering on shock.

"I-I don't know what happened. We were talking and one m-minute he w-was fine and the n-next . . . H-he just . . . I don't kn-know what happened."

"Shh. It's okay." Dammit all to hell. I knew something like this was going to happen.

Something I'd been trying to avoid for months, but Kiernan refused to step up. She deserved better. "Dammit. I *told* him. I told him to tell you before something like this happened."

"Tell me what?" Jade sucked her lower lip into her mouth to stop the quivering and my gut clenched. "You knew this was going to happen?"

This wasn't fair. She deserved the truth. All of it. *Now.* "Take a walk with me. We need to talk. This shit has gone on long enough."

Mom was still having no luck with the woman behind the desk. "Ma'am I already told you, the doctor will come out to see you when—"

"I understand that, but I don't want to see the doctor. I want to see my *son*!"

"Mom?"

Immediately dismissing the nurse's response—a textbook answer she'd probably delivered a thousand times, herself—Mom swung her attention around to the second best thing she could get. Her *other* son. Her bloodshot eyes shifted from me, to Jade, and back again. She knew what had to happen.

"I'm taking Jade for a walk. I'm telling her. Everything."

ANGEL

Mom's tear stained cheeks almost changed my mind. She needed me. But so did Jade. So did Kiernan, for that matter, but I was only one person. I couldn't be everywhere for everyone, all the time. I needed to prioritize. Shoving aside the inevitable guilt that came with my decision, I led Jade out onto the busy sidewalk. Wheelchairs carted patients to and from cars, a young girl struggled with crutches beside an older man carrying a 'Get Well' balloon. Horns honked, sirens wailed, babies cried. It wasn't exactly the ideal spot for a leisurely stroll. Or the ideal weather. I hadn't even noticed the icy wind on my way there, or the fact that I'd neglected to bring a jacket, but now it whipped around us, tossing Jade's hair in her face and numbing my fingers.

Luckily, we had other options.

"I thought we were walking?" Jade blinked up at me as I held open the back door of my car for her.

"Too damn cold. Get in. We can sit and talk here."

She shimmied over and I contorted my body in order to fit between the front seats to reach the ignition. It took a few blind jabs, but I managed to plant the key and get the heat flowing from the vents in the dash. A few minutes, some serious fiddling, and a possible hernia later, the warm air was blowing steadily into the back.

When I'd run out of excuses to stall, I collapsed into my seat and tried to figure out how the hell I was supposed to do this.

I could still remember the doctor who first told us that Kiernan's tumor was inoperable. I remembered everything about him, from the crooked shape of his nose, to the exact shade of brown of his eyes, to the mole on his upper neck just below his left ear. I doubted I'd ever erase his face from my mind. The way his lips moved around the words that destroyed all hope. And I hated him. It was completely irrational. None of what he told us was his fault, but I hated him for being the one to tell us. For being the one to cause that kind of unbearable pain.

I didn't want to be the one to do that to her. I didn't want Jade to hate me. As selfish as it made me, I wanted Kiernan's face to be the one attached to this god-awful memory, not mine.

"Dammit. It should be Kiernan telling you this. You deserve that much from him, but enough is enough." I don't know where I found the strength to look at her, but it was the least I could do. Look her in the eye as I tore out her heart and stomped on it. "I don't want to be the one to do this, but you need to know. Jade . . . Kiernan's sick."

Jade arched one narrow brow and cast a pointed look at the Emergency Room sign standing not more than ten feet from where I'd parked. I wasn't being clear.

No, I was being an outright coward.

"I'm not talking flu sick. He's . . ." Hearing it was going to wound her. *Deeply*. But saying it out loud wasn't much easier. I steeled myself for the impact and then let the truth tumble from my lips. "He's terminal."

I expected her to cry. Or scream. Or, who knows, hit me maybe? Any one of them would have been understandable reactions. She did none. Stronger than I gave her credit for, she fought back the natural tears that wanted to escape and locked them away. But she was using that strength in all the wrong ways.

"No."

"It's okay, Jade." She had to know that she didn't need to hide from me. That I could take whatever she needed to dish out.

"No. No, it's not." Despite her best efforts, a few rogue tears managed to overflow and trickle down her flushed cheeks. She scrubbed roughly at her soon to be raw skin.

"Stop." It broke my heart to break hers. To watch her try so hard to take all of that pain I'd caused her and bottle it up. Cuffing her wrists, I tugged until she relented and allowed me to lower them from her face. "It's okay *to cry*. He is dying, Jade. Kiernan is going to die. Sooner rather than later. You can deny it all you want, but it's going to happen. You need to be prepared for that."

She needed to know—not only that, but *accept*—the truth. It was the only hope she stood of defending herself. So, I pushed her. I pushed her mercilessly toward the harsh reality, feeling every bit the bastard I was along the way. I pushed and pushed . . . until she broke. Absolutely shattered in my arms.

And, because I wasn't already a big enough asshole, I held her.

ANGEL

She clung to me like a life raft in a storm, but she was wrong. I wasn't the life raft, I was the hurricane. Destroying everything in my path. In the face of her grief, my own resurfaced. Raw and bitter. Forced into submission for so long that I could barely contain the outpouring of it, now.

Long overdue tears streamed silently down my face as I clutched her tightly to my chest. I was five-years-old again and she was my stuffed bear. I was playing the big, bad protector, but the truth was, I was drawing my strength from her. She stayed there, allowing me to fill my role. Supporting me. Alleviating not one ounce of the guilt that weighed heavily on my heart.

My own tears had dried by the time her sobs turned to hiccups and eventually quieted altogether. Still, she made no attempt to move. I could have held her like that forever. Some small place inside of me seemed to quiet with her near. A measure of peace I hadn't felt in a long, long time. But that was wrong. My brother—her *boyfriend*—was lying in a hospital bed, waiting for us.

I cleared away the lump in my throat and tilted my head to get a better look at her. "You ready?"

She nodded. Dark hair whispering softly against my chin, rubbing against the day-old stubble, making it itch.

"Alright." Removing my arms felt like trying to pry open a padlock with my bare hands. I didn't want to let her go.

Bitter wind stung my cheeks the moment we climbed out of the car, cluing me in to the fact that they weren't as dry as I thought they were. I ducked into the front seat to grab my keys and watched Jade take a steadying breath as I used a shirt sleeve to clean up my own face.

"Jade?" My finger came dangerously close to getting shut in the door, but I barely noticed when she turned to look at me. The oceans of heartache churning in her eyes were enough to make me want to crawl in a hole somewhere. I could only imagine what that look would do to Kiernan. Seeing her in that kind of pain was going to gut him. "Kiernan's scared. I know he doesn't look like he is, or act like he is, but he's my brother and I'm telling you, *he is*. And I think what terrifies him most is hurting you. He's going to need us to be strong for him. Do you understand?"

ANGEL

She understood. Her head came up, shoulders back, and she rearranged her facial features into that perfect mask I knew oh-so-well. The thing about knowing that mask was that I was painfully aware of exactly what kind of hurt lay hidden underneath. The staggering amount of agony that could be concealed by a smile.

"I just want him to find peace, Jade, and he won't be able to do that if he doesn't think you'll be okay. If he thinks he's making you suffer."

"I understand." She turned to go, but I couldn't let her leave. Not yet. She thought she understood, but she didn't. She couldn't. *I* didn't even understand.

I felt like I was being torn in two. Incapable of choosing a side. Half of me wanted to shield my little brother from anything bad, which included Jade's pain. He was my brother. That was my job. But that meant forcing her to bury that pain. To do what I'd been doing for months, keeping it locked away inside, slowly eating at you, decaying chunks of your soul, while the outward shell remained intact.

The other half of me was disgusted at the thought of doing that to her. To this beautiful angel with far too much pain already tearing her down. How could I ask her to bear more? Suffering silently, alone, in the dark, the way I did?

"Wait." I snatched her wrist before she could get away. Such a tiny wrist. I could feel all of the bones. It felt almost fragile in my powerful grasp, like if I squeezed even a little, I'd crush it. That's what it felt like I was doing to her. Crushing her. Standing that close, it was hard not to notice how small she was. In every way. How . . . vulnerable. Why did this have to be so damn hard? "I . . . I want you know it's okay to hurt, though. Just not in front of Kiernan. Being strong for someone when you're falling apart inside is one of the hardest things there is. Believe me, I know. It's not fair to put this on you, and I'm sorry. If you ever need to talk, or cry, or wail on something with a baseball bat, come find me. Any time. Call me in the middle of the night when it really hits you, because it will. I'll be there for you. I promise. We'll get through this together, okay?"

She took a moment to collect herself and this time when she nodded, I knew she was ready. I knew she could do it for the same reason I could.

Because we *had* to.

Eight

"Hey, bro. Lookin' good."

Kiernan scowled back at me from where he sat partially reclined on the mechanical bed in his too-hot-to-handle white hospital gown with the little blue and red polka dots.

"Leave your brother alone." Mom rooted through an overnight bag she kept in her trunk packed with some of Kiernan's things for situations such as these. "He's had a rough day."

Pulling out a pair of old sweats and a t-shirt, she handed them over to Kiernan, who looked at them like they were made of pure gold. "Thanks, Mom."

He scooted over to the side of the bed, only to be barricaded by her body. "Did the doctor clear you to get out of that bed?"

"Mom," Kiernan groaned and rolled his eyes. "What am I supposed to do? Change here?"

"Wait until the doctor moves you to a private room."

"That could take *hours*."

"Kiernan—"

"Mom . . ." As much as I was enjoying the show, I took pity on the poor kid. Jade was anxious to see him and somehow I doubted he wanted her in the audience for his drag show. "Let him go change in the bathroom. It'll only take a minute and I'll go with him."

"What will the doctor say?" Mom folded her arms and tipped her head. She was a formidable woman, but when faced with the united front of her sons, she usually caved.

"Nothing. What's he going to do? Tell Kiernan to get up *again* to go change back into the gown? No."

I let her stew on that for a minute until she huffed a dramatic sigh. A clear sign we'd won. Celebrating too soon was the only thing that could ruin this for us now, so Kiernan and I both remained stone faced until she announced her surrender. "Oh, fine. Go ahead, then. But make it quick."

"Thanks, Mom." Kiernan pecked her lightly on the cheek as he slid past her.

Dizziness is a common side effect of seizures. After Kiernan's first seizure, he regained consciousness before the EMTs arrived and tried to stand up. He ended up with a pretty nasty bruise on his forehead. Probably why Mom was so keen on keeping him in that bed. Definitely why I followed behind him close enough to be considered harassment.

He made it past nurses and aids, almost to the bathroom door at the end of the hall before stumbling. Another benefit of my invasion of his personal space was that I blocked their view as I steadied him with a hand on his shoulder and shoved him through the door.

Recovering quickly, Kiernan scurried into the first stall to change his clothes before Mom changed her mind.

"So . . ." I couldn't see him, but that didn't mean I was done keeping an eye on him. Or at the very least, an ear. "What happened?"

"I don't know." One foot disappeared from beneath the stall door and I heard a bang as he hopped around. "I was at this writing workshop with Jade and—"

The foot reappeared and all movement stopped inside the stall. "Shit . . . Jade."

I was wondering how long it would take him to connect-the-dots. "Yeah."

Silence permeated the cold room, broken only by the continued sounds of Kiernan struggling to dress in confined quarters.

The door swung inward and Kiernan's pale face stared at me through his reflection in the mirror. "Please tell me she wasn't in the ambulance, at least."

My silence was all the answer he needed.

Kiernan groaned and shoved the gown into the trash bin beside the sinks. "Is she okay?"

"She'll be alright. She was scared, but what do you expect?"

Guilt blanketed the room. "You told her, didn't you?"

"I had to."

Bracing himself against the cold porcelain of the sink, Kiernan shut his eyes and let his head fall forward. "Did I break her heart? Am I the biggest jerk on the planet?"

"No. You're a scared kid, dealing with a lot of really serious shit, and having to make some really tough decisions."

"But I made all the wrong ones. I should have told her. I should have listened to you. It should have been *me*. You kept telling me to tell her, I just . . . I just kept thinking I had more time, ya know? One more day?" His tone flooded with resignation. "But I didn't. And I put it on you, instead. I know you didn't want to be the one to hurt her. I'm sorry."

"What's done is done, Kiernan. You can Monday morning quarterback it all you want. It's not going to change a thing. What matters is that she knows, now. And she's still sitting out there, waiting to see you. She's *still here*, Kier."

Straightening, he flipped on the faucet and washed his hands. "Do you think they'll let her in to see me?"

"Technically, it's family only. But you know Mom. They'll let Jade in."

He nodded absently as he balled the paper towel and tossed it in the trash. "I need to talk to her. I need to explain. And apologize. And . . ."

"I don't think any of that is neces—"

"What if it's too much for her?" True fear—the kind I'd only seen from Kiernan a handful of times throughout all of this—flashed in his eyes. "She's dealing with so much, Cal. You have no idea."

I thought I had a pretty good idea, actually, but I kept my mouth shut.

"It's like all of this *stuff* has been weighing on her for years—her whole life—causing tiny stress fractures all the way down to her foundation. What if this is the final blow that brings it all crumbling down? What if *I* end up destroying her?"

"Take a breath, bro." Nausea rolled over me as he put voice to my deepest fears, but I wouldn't let him see that. Kiernan was practically panting with anxiety. If I brought him back to that room stressed out and worked up, they'd never let him leave that bed again. "I think you're giving yourself too much credit. And Jade, too little. She's stronger than you think. Jade's a tough girl. She'll get through this."

"I know." I was glad to see him take a calming breath and release it slowly. "I know she is. I just . . . I wanted to be the one to help her.

Why can't I be the one to help her hold it all together?"

"You *can*. Kiernan, just because she knows the truth doesn't mean anything has to change. She still needs you. A blind man could see how much you mean to her. You love her. She loves you. Don't waste that. And don't waste time. It's too precious."

Kiernan nodded. "You're right."

"I usually am." A self-amused smirk curled my lips.

I know Kiernan heard me because he shook his head at me, but he continued as though I hadn't spoken. "Can you get her? Send her in?"

"I can. But you'd better get your butt back in that bed before Mom needs to be admitted."

Kiernan tried and failed to hide a yawn behind a smile. "Don't worry. If we're the cause of Mom getting admitted, it won't be to the emergency room. It'll be the psych ward."

***

For the longest time, I stood there watching her. Jade looked exhausted, slumped sideways in her seat as though gravity itself had grown too strong a force for her to resist. The weight of the truth weighing her down. Grounding her into the dirt. It had been a long, emotional day for us all. She was fading fast, and she hadn't even faced the hardest part of it, yet.

"Hey." I slid into the chair beside her, carefully searching her face for signs of shock. I never should have left her alone out there. Her eyes were damp, but clear and alert. Leftover tears lingered on her cheeks, but otherwise her skin was dry. Not cold or clammy. And her breathing appeared to be even. "He wants to see you. Are you going to be alright?"

"I'll hold it together." The transformation was practically instantaneous. The shields slamming into place. Her tumultuous gaze locking down and staring back at me with an almost deadly calm. The strong perfume of sadness that hung heavy in the air around her only moments earlier dissipated until barely a whiff remained.

"I know. I'm not worried about that." Her shields were impenetrable. It was what was happening behind those shields that concerned me. "I'm worried about *you*."

"I'll be fine." She didn't look any more convinced of that statement than I was.

ANGEL

"I told him that you know. He wasn't thrilled that I was the one to tell you, but he understands why I had to. He's really sorry that he didn't tell you sooner."

"I'm not mad at him, if that's what you're worried about."

"I already told you what I'm worried about."

"And I told you, I'm fine. What room is he in?" She may have come across as snippy to anyone else, but I knew what the problem was. Beyond the obvious stress she was under, Jade wasn't used to having anyone worry about her. She didn't know how to react to it.

She practically vibrated with nervous energy the whole way down the hall. And when Mom emerged and pulled her into a hug, it was clear she wasn't used to that, either.

Mom was in tears. Jade's eyes were misting over. I needed to separate them before we ended up with a mess on our hands. "Alright, enough, Mom. You don't want to turn her into a blubbering mess before she even gets through the door."

I wrapped an arm around Mom's shoulders, easing her away from Jade. "Let's give them some time. Go ahead."

Jade reached for the doorknob, but all of that nervous energy had abandoned her. She looked unsure of herself and more than a little frightened. Understandable. The last she'd seen Kiernan, he'd been unconscious in the back of an ambulance. She had no idea what waited on the other side of that door.

Mom headed back toward the waiting room as my hand closed over Jade's shoulder. "It's just Kiernan. And he just wants to see his girlfriend. You'll be fine, remember?"

She nodded with a confidence I knew she couldn't feel and reached again. This time she made the final leap across the threshold and I watched the door swing shut behind her.

Mom was plugging away on her phone when I caught up to her. Her yellow scrubs with the tiny blue moons, crumpled and unkempt. She'd been in the middle of a double shift when Kiernan was brought in. The tidy ponytail she always wore to work had come loose and hung in tangles around her shoulders from having her hands run through it so many times. Even her makeup had been wiped away along with her tears.

ANGEL

Sighing, she leaned against the waiting room wall and shut her eyes.

"Why don't you go home, Mom? You look tired."

"Gee, thanks, Cal." Her smile was weak, but genuine.

"You know what I mean. It's been a long day. The doctor already said Kiernan won't be released until morning. You might as well get some rest until then."

"What about you? Are you heading home now?" Mom reached for her purse and started fishing around inside.

"Figured I'd hang around here until Jade's ready and drop her off at home on my way."

"That's very thoughtful of you." Dangling her car keys, she zipped up the bag. "How late do you think you'll be?"

"I don't know. Visiting hours are almost over."

"Mmhmm." She nodded absently, her eyes glued to the door, behind which Kiernan was struggling to comfort Jade, while she struggled to do the same for him. "Alright, then. I'll see you in a bit. And please tell Jade I said good night."

"I will." Watching Mom shuffle toward the exit, it struck me that she didn't stand quite as tall as she used to.

***

The sun sank low, casting a bright orange glare through the oversized windows that made up the entire west wall of the Emergency Department. My ass was going numb in the hard, plastic chairs waiting for Jade. I knew they had a lot to talk about and that it would take time to sort through it all, but I was anxious to see the end result. To fast-forward and *know* that they would both be alright. The *not knowing* was causing some serious damage to my blood pressure.

The glare had diminished to little more than a glow on the horizon by the time she reemerged.

"Hey." I stood and met her halfway. "How was it?"

"It was . . . better than I expected." Her fingers twisted tightly in the dark hair falling over her shoulder. "He seems so . . . normal. Like nothing's wrong."

"Yeah. I know. It can be so easy to forget sometimes. But you can't. You can't let yourself forget. Otherwise, you have to deal with the remembering part. And that sucks."

"Good point." Her fingers broke free from the strands of dark silk strangling them and she immediately started in on her poor nails.

"Do you have a ride home?"

"Um . . ." What was left of her fingernails were saved when she ripped her hand away from her mouth and shoved it in her pocket. "I figured I'd just call a cab." Her hand shifted around her pocket and she frowned. "Or walk. It's not that far and—"

"It's dark, Jade. You're not walking home. And I'm sure as hell not letting you waste your money on a cab when I have a perfectly good car just sitting in the lot."

She was crazy if she thought I was letting her walk in those sub-arctic temperatures. She wouldn't have made it five feet. The icy wind chased leaves across the darkened lot, scattering paper products and flapping Jade's jacket against her waist,

We drove in silence for a while. Not an awkward silence—where no one knows what to say, but everyone feels like they have to say something. A comfortable silence. The kind that brought out a sense of peace in me that I hadn't felt all day. All *year*. Outside of the pool. Being with Jade was like being underwater in all of the good ways. And some of the bad. There was something about being around her that made it difficult to breathe, but it was a sacrifice I was willing to make.

"Caulder?" She'd been working up the courage to say whatever she had to say for most of the ride. Evidently, she'd found it. I only wished it hadn't taken her so long.

I made her nervous. That had to change. "Cal."

"What?"

"You can call me Cal." Not many people did. Kiernan and our parents, that was about it. But I liked the idea of adding Jade's name to that list.

"Oh . . . Cal?"

Yeah, I definitely liked it. "Hmm?"

"Can I ask you a dumb question?"

"Sure." The light we'd been stopped at turned green and I rolled forward, wishing it had stayed red a little longer.

ANGEL

"What should I do tomorrow?" Jade frowned the moment she finished speaking and I could practically see the internal eye roll that wasn't there. "I mean, I know Kiernan's being released, and I'm assuming you're taking him back home, and—"

"Stop." Screw traffic lights. There wasn't another car in sight and I could stop where I damn well pleased. Swerving onto the shoulder, I threw the car in park and twisted to get a better look at her chewing fiercely at that lip again. "That's not a dumb question, Jade. It's not easy to know what the right thing is in situations like these. You don't want to overwhelm Kiernan, you don't want to impose on family time. All that shows is that you care. You're considerate and you have a good heart. There's nothing dumb about that."

I waited until she had a chance to process that. Her fingers unwound in her lap and she released her battered lip. Satisfied she'd heard me, I pulled back onto the road and continued toward her place.

It didn't elude me that I'd failed to actually answer her question, but the truth was only she could answer that. And it was an answer that held more weight for me than I liked to admit.

Like a sissy, I waited until we were parked outside her building—where I could make a quick getaway—before giving it to her.

"I guess it comes down to what *you* want to do. Don't worry about overwhelming Kiernan. He doesn't have a lot of time left and he wants to spend every moment of it with the people he loves. That includes you. Mom and I have had a year to come to grips with this. I'm afraid you won't have that much time. So the question is, what do you want to do with it?"

She didn't even hesitate. "Spend it with Kiernan."

And that was it. *That* was the moment I knew my prayers had been answered. I was right all along. She *was* the angel my brother needed her to be.

She was the angel we all needed.

Nine

The highway stretched out before me as far as my headlights could reach. Beyond that, the darkness seemed strangely inviting. The unknown, the unseen. The obscurity. I could disappear out there. Hide from everyone and everything. I could feel those dark thoughts creeping up on me, so I shut my brain down and functioned on auto-pilot.

After making sure Jade was safely inside her building, I'd had every intention of going home. But my wheels kept on turning and now I was miles from town. Windows cracked to let in fresh air. Heater cranked to fight of the chill. Radio blasting to drown out any and every thought. Hours ticked by. I had to stop for gas. I sang along with the classic rock station until my throat ached and my voice broke.

I needed a break and this was the only way I knew how to find one. The urge to toss my cell and never turn around was powerful. It would be so easy to run. Leave it all behind. Dad had done it.

But I wasn't him. I wasn't a coward. I was stronger than that. At least I hoped I was, because if I wasn't, I'd die trying to be.

Pulling onto the shoulder, I snapped off the radio. The sudden silence pounded in my ears as thoughts slowly snaked their way back in. Reminders of what I couldn't forget. I squared my shoulders as that weight I'd been trying to outrun settled back on them.

Break time over.

The house was dark when I parked in the drive. Not unexpected. Mom was home, but it was late. After eleven. I should have called her. She was probably worried by now. I could have at least—

Dry, gasping sobs reverberated through the darkened rooms, assaulting my ears the moment I opened the door. Shrill, cackling misery, drowning out my thoughts.

"Mom?" I followed the gut-wrenching sounds to the kitchen.

ANGEL

She lay in a crumpled heap on soaking wet tiles, a bucket of soapy water beside her. A yellow sponge was still gripped tightly in one fist.

"*Mom!*"

Her entire body shook with the sheer force of her grief.

"Mom, it's okay. I'm here, now." What the hell was I thinking leaving her alone after the day she'd had? Prying the sponge from her vice-like fingers, I tossed it into the bucket and pulled her onto my lap. "Shh. It's alright."

One thing that couldn't be said about my father was that he was a deadbeat. Despite being absent from our lives in every way, he did send those checks every month. And more than just child support for Kiernan. A *lot* more. Mom didn't need to be on her hands and knees, scrubbing a floor. She wanted to be. It was her coping mechanism of choice. Always had been. Which didn't bother me in the least.

Until tonight.

Even with only the moon's pale light filtering through the large bay window, I could see how red and raw her hands looked. Tortured for hours by unknown chemicals and cleaning supplies.

For a long time, I thought it was her way of getting a little privacy. Kiernan and I saw housework and we generally went in the opposite direction. But this was something else, entirely. This was my mother punishing herself. Because there was no one else to punish.

It shook me right down to my foundation. This woman—this insubstantial body—wailing with misery, clinging to me in desperation. This was my mother. My *mom*. The strongest person in the world. The person I'd looked up to my entire life. The woman who had held me, and loved me, and rocked me as a child. The woman who had cheered me on and supported every decision I'd ever made, right or wrong. The woman who taught me about the type of person I wanted to be. *That* woman was falling apart right before my eyes.

I wished I could reverse time. Go back to when I was the one who cried in her arms. When all sorrows could be healed with a kiss and a popsicle. I wasn't her little boy, anymore. Her little boy was lying in a hospital bed. And I was there. Holding her together, while she fell apart.

ANGEL

The weight of responsibility settled firmly on my chest, squeezing the air from my lungs. A deep, painful ache clenched the back of my throat and the sting of tears forced my eyes shut.

"Please, Mom. I'm here. I'm right here." But *I* would never be enough. No matter what I did. No matter what I said. Kiernan would leave us. And when that happened, I'd never be enough to fill the hole it left in her heart. "I'm sorry, Mom. I'm so sorry."

And it broke. The solid cement casing around my heart splintered into a thousand pieces, slicing my insides like shrapnel. "I'm so sorry. I'm so sorry."

A black cloud settled over us. With each breath, I drew it in. Felt it filling up that hollow place inside of me with cold, unrelenting darkness. I knew that darkness. I'd been fighting it off day and night for over a year. But my defenses were down. I'd shown a moment of weakness. And it wasted no time invading.

The darkness had thorns and needles and claws and fangs. It shredded me from the inside out. Tearing away at my heart, my soul, my flesh. The pain was excruciating.

I wanted to scream, but the sound died on my parted lips. I needed to cry. To weep and wail like my mother. To find some sort of release. A way to spit out the vile blackness devouring me. But the tears wouldn't come. The agony, the fury, the bitterness, the grief. All of it, caged so tightly, would never find an escape. It would only grow and grow until I couldn't contain it anymore. And then . . . Then, we were all in trouble.

Silent shudders wracked my tormented body. As the moon sailed silently across the window, I fought a private battle against my despair, while Mom surrendered to hers. When she grew heavy against my chest, I knew that exhaustion had finally won out.

Scooping her into my arms, I struggled up the stairs. I felt weak. As though someone had pulled a plug and drained all of the strength from me, body and soul. The day had taken its toll and left me broke. I had nothing more to give.

After tucking Mom into her own bed, I dragged my feet down the hall. My phone clattered to the floor as I stripped off my jeans and a pale blue, pulsing light filled the room, indicating the *seven* missed calls I had. All from Beth.

ANGEL

Dammit. The study group. I was completely screwed.

The shadows of my bedroom closed in around me. Suffocating me. Crushing me. How much longer could I do this? How much longer could I go on like this? I was running on empty and saw no end in sight.

The sound of Mom's cries mingled with Jade's in the silent room. So much heartbreak. So much misery.

And above it all, came the sound of my own sorrow.

"I'm so sorry I'm not enough."

Ten

We'd been home from the hospital for less than an hour and the mood in the house had plummeted to somewhere in the neighborhood of morose. Mom was locked in her office, avoiding me I assumed given that she hadn't been able to look me in the eye all morning. And Kiernan was up in his room, listening to some kind of emo music. On a loop.

I was so sick of the seemingly requisite moping that came along with each and every reminder of Kiernan's condition. It's not like we ever managed to forget about it, but each time something like this happened it felt like we all needed to go through a period of mourning. Why? He wasn't dead. Wasn't that something to be celebrated?

ANGEL

And yet, the house was every bit the depressing scene I was certain Jade feared she'd be walking into any minute. Well, screw that.

"Mom?" I knocked on her door and waited for her to open it. She couldn't avoid me forever.

"Cal?" Her hair was arranged in perfect curls cascading around her shoulders and she'd spent hours on her makeup. She wore a pressed outfit that I rarely saw outside of special events and a set of matching, delicate jewelry. Every line, every button, every curl in place. As though she needed to prove to . . . Me? Her? Everyone? That she was still in control after losing it the night before. "Did you need something?"

"Yeah. I was thinking . . . We skipped breakfast this morning, and Kiernan's had nothing but hospital food since yesterday . . . Jade's coming over and she's never had your stew. Maybe you could make some for lunch?"

Asking Mom if she wanted to cook was like asking a golden retriever if it wanted to play fetch. The definition of a dumb question. When her eyes finally reached mine and I saw that light in them I hadn't seen in two days, I knew I'd nailed it.

"That's a wonderful idea." She turned back into her office, leaving the door open, and I watched her power down her computer. "I should have all of the ingredients I need, but if not I'll make a quick run to the store. Why don't you see if you can get your brother to come downstairs while I raid the pantry?"

"Sure." Dragging Kiernan's butt out of bed had been next on my to-do list, anyway.

Sticking his favorite video game in the console—the one I spent far too much time practicing, while he was at school—I cranked the volume and headed upstairs. I needed something up my sleeve to lure him out of isolation at times like these, and his competitive nature usually did the trick.

"Hey. How are you feeling?"

Kiernan groaned and pulled a pillow over his head. "Tired. And if one more person asks me that, I'm going to—"

"Too tired to get your ass kicked? Again?" This was going to go one of two ways. Either, he really was too tired to give in to my taunting, in which case I'd have to call Jade and tell her to come over some other time. Something I really didn't want to have to do to her. Or his ego would outrank his fatigue.

I had to suppress a grin when he tossed the pillow aside to glare at me. "You only won last time because I—"

"Excuses, excuses. Think you can beat me?"

"I know I can."

"Prove it."

Kiernan was on his feet and out the door ahead of me. I grinned at his back the whole way downstairs.

His favorite blue controller was already on the sofa where he always sat and I left him scrolling through the menu of customizable options when the doorbell rang. I knew exactly what he was looking for. The AK-47. He was nothing if not predictable. No appreciation for the subtler things in life. One day, I was going to take him and his assault rifle out with a pocket knife. Just to prove I could.

"Jade." Wide, startled eyes stared back at me when I opened the door. Her gaze darted down the hall behind me, where an atomic sounding blast shook the frames. "Come on! You're just in time to watch me kick Kiernan's butt."

With rapid gun fire blasting through the house, we didn't bother trying to talk anymore until we reached the media room. Evidently, she hadn't yet been introduced to my favorite room in the house because she stood there, gaping at the enormous flat screen on the wall.

"Jade!" Kiernan's eyes never left the game until his final foe was defeated and he threw a victory fist into the air. "Perfect timing. You can watch me pulverize Cal."

Jade's eyes flicked from Kiernan, to me, around the room, and back to Kiernan again while her mouth opened and closed around unspoken words. She wasn't prepared for this. *Idiot.* I'd just dropped the emotional equivalent of a nuclear bomb on her and now I expected her to act like nothing had changed? Like everything was—?

"Funny." The lopsided tip of her lips shocked the hell out of me as she flopped down beside Kiernan. "Cal just claimed something very similar."

"Did he now? Well, we'll have to see who's right." Kiernan leaned in for a quick kiss. Nothing weird about that. Except the way Jade's gaze cut to me the moment they parted.

ANGEL

Who the hell appointed me chaperone?

It was the last time she looked at me all morning. She wasn't shutting me out on purpose. She'd simply built this protective bubble around her and Kiernan, and everyone outside of it had ceased to exist. All things considered, it wasn't unreasonable, but I'd be lying if I said that coldness inside of me didn't grow just a little more bitter.

"Here. Why don't you give it a shot?"

Jade's eyes locked on the controller in my outstretched hand before lifting to mine. It was worth forfeiting my record breaking winning streak for that moment of her warmth. A single look and that solid block of ice in my chest began to thaw.

"Are you sure? I'm sure I'll be terrible. I've never—"

"You'll never know until you try. Besides, it looks like Kiernan could use a little *less* competition."

A throw pillow sailed past my head and I burst out laughing. "Your aim is just as bad in real life, bro."

Another pillow went flying with the same atrocious results and the smile on Jade's face was enough to heat me all the way through.

Kiernan proceeded to massacre her seven straight rounds. By the eighth, she'd stopped spinning in circles every time she tried to turn around and actually managed to get a few shots off. They all hit the wall, but that wasn't the point. She was so bad, she *couldn't* have been having fun, but she kept on playing—entertaining Kiernan and I to no end—until Kiernan finally took pity on her and declared it lunch time.

"Perfect timing, stew's almost ready." Mom waved us into the kitchen where thick meaty scents made my stomach sit up and take notice. "Why don't you boys set the table and see if Jade would like something to drink?"

I pulled out the set of old stone bowls Grandma had given us back when Mom and Dad first got married. They weren't really fancy, but they were sentimental, and they had this cool berry design that I never in a million years would have admitted out-loud that I liked.

The glasses were just that: glass with some flowery engravings that I was proud to say held

no interest for me. I passed those over to
Kiernan, who was busy giving Jade a tour of our
refrigerator. "While you're at it, I'll take some
lemonade."

Jade looked . . . fascinated. By what? Soda? I
didn't ask. I didn't want to know. I had a feeling
the answer would only piss me off.

I handed the dishes to Mom, who stood over
her cauldron sized pot, ladle in hand. Looked like
we'd be eating stew for a week. Maybe we could
send some home with—

My thoughts were derailed by the sound of
breaking glass.

"Oh crap. I'm sorry." Kiernan leapt for the
paper towels as a puddle of lemonade pooled
around Jade's feet, the spray covering her shoes
and halfway up her pant legs. "You okay?"

"Yeah, I'm fine."

I crouched in front of her, secretly examining
her legs for any signs of bleeding, while I swept
up the shattered debris. Jade appeared to be fine.
Kiernan, less so. I could hear him shuffling
around behind me, not knowing what to do, what
to say.

"Are *you* okay?" Jade's gaze zeroed in on Kiernan's hand, which was flexing and fisting by his side.

"I'm good." The hand disappeared into his pocket with one of those lackluster grins, and I fought the urge to slap him upside the head.

It was bullshit and I knew it. Worse, *Jade* knew it. Nothing serious, just some muscle weakness that came and went from time to time, but he was lying to her about it. And he had to be blind if he couldn't see the way that hurt her.

***

We followed lunch with a marathon of some of Kiernan's favorite movies. The kind that made the house shake with the sheer volume of the massive explosions taking place on screen. Not Jade's usual genre of choice, I was sure, but she didn't complain. She just laid there beside my brother and fought to keep her eyes open for as long as possible. Not long after she lost her battle with exhaustion, Kiernan surrendered, as well.

The movie continued to play, but I couldn't tear my eyes away from them long enough to keep up with whatever was going on. It was probably a creepy thing to do, watching them sleep, but I couldn't help myself. Whenever I looked at either of them it was impossible not to see the weight they carried. Silent struggles waged in each of them for different reasons, but they both fought every moment they were awake. Maybe it's what drew them together in the first place. But now, in sleep, they both looked . . . peaceful.

I wondered about Kiernan. If when the end finally came, if he'd have that kind of peace always. No more fear. No more pain. No more struggles.

And I wondered about Jade. If she'd ever find it.

I prayed for both of them that the answer was yes.

Eleven

When you start to confuse the effects of mitosis and fibrosis, you know you're in trouble. And that's exactly where I was—*deep*—as I watched the final few minutes of the mid-term tick by, staring at a blank essay question.

I was already so far behind and this was just another step in the wrong direction. Sometimes I wondered why I bothered at all. My entire freshman year was wasted on business classes I thought I'd need until I switched majors. I didn't get to complete my second semester sophomore year because of the move. And now I was trying to make that up by taking classes I was just going to have to retake again later, anyway. What was the point? At this rate, I'd be a corpse before I'd be a doctor.

ANGEL

"Time's up. Leave your exams on my desk on your way out." The professor leaned against the board and scanned the room as students began filing down the stairs to drop off their test papers.

The guy couldn't have been more than a few years older than me and it made me seriously question what I was doing wrong. How was it that he stood up there with all the answers, while I sat here with none? What had gone so right in his life, or so *wrong* in mine, to make that the case?

There was only one answer I could come up with, and I hated myself for it.

"Caulder!" Beth squeezed her way through the line to catch up with me as I neared the bottom, trailed closely by Marjorie. "Hey. Glad that's over, huh?"

"Yeah." At least it couldn't get any worse.

"We're going to The Post tonight with some people to celebrate." Beth collected my test along with the two Marjorie carried and stacked them all neatly on the professor's desk as we filed by. "You wanna come?"

The Post was your typical college town bar: loud, rowdy, and crowded. Not my usual scene, but tonight it sounded like the perfect place to get my mind off more depressing things. "Sure. What time?"

"Around nine?"

"Sounds good."

Marjorie winked at Beth, earning herself a stiff jab of Beth's elbow in return. "Great. See ya there."

***

There was a reason I'd only been to The Post once before. Once was once more than enough. And twice . . . That was just stupidity. A bunch of drunken idiots bumping into each other and spilling drinks everywhere. And it wasn't even ten, yet.

I was running late. Beth had texted me while I was driving to let me know they were all there and seated in a booth near the corner. I dodged three teetering girls in short shorts and belly shirts, and took the long way around what looked like the making of a bar brawl waiting to happen, scanning table after table for a familiar face.

ANGEL

Bartenders shouted, people laughed and hollered, and the music pumped loudly enough to rattle the floor boards.

"Caulder! *Caulder,* over here!" It was Marjorie's red hair that I spotted first, though it was Beth who was waving me down.

Relieved just to escape the madhouse of the dance floor, I slid onto the torn plastic chair beside Beth. "Hey. It's crazy in here."

"Yeah. It's usually too much for me, but every once and a while you gotta cut loose and blow off some steam. This is a great place to do it. Mainly because everyone's too drunk to remember anything you did or said the next morning."

I laughed along with her. "Good point."

"Hi, Caulder." Marjorie was grinning at us across the battered wooden table. The thing had probably had more alcohol poured on it than the lining of an alcoholics stomach.

"Hey, Marjorie." I made the round of 'hellos' to everyone else at the table. Tom, Alex, and Ashley from class, and two other girls I didn't recognize.

"What do you want to drink? The waitress comes by about once a year, so you have to grab her when you can."

"Um . . ." I wasn't a stranger to the bar scene. Back in Cali, I'd set sail with Captain Morgan more times than I cared to remember. And I was sure there were a few that I couldn't. But things were different now. My priorities had shifted. And I'd had an up-close and personal look at the other side of alcohol. What it could do to a person, and what that could do to the people in that person's life. "I think I'll stick with water."

"You sure?" I'd swear Beth looked almost disappointed. "I thought we were blowing off steam tonight."

"Probably not a good idea." Even if I could find a way to blow off steam, I'd likely take the roof with me.

"What?" Beth leaned in closer, her shoulder bumping against my arm, and tilted her head to better hear me.

"Nothing. Never mind. What are you drinking? I can make a run up to the bar."

"Brave man." Marjorie giggled and slid her empty glass to me. Not her first refill, I was guessing. "I'll take a rum and coke."

ANGEL

"An amaretto sour, please." Beth flashed a smile as I gathered up her empty cup, as well, and extracted myself from the relative safety of the table.

What the hell was I thinking? No bottle of water was worth all of this. Chaos surrounded the bar, people jockeying for position with no rhyme or reason. Everyone out for themselves, not giving a damn who they had to step on to get what they wanted. It was a zoo.

When I finally managed to hail someone down with the use of actual coherent language skills, I ordered the drinks and dropped a couple twenties on the bar. There was a snowballs chance in hell I was sticking around to wait for change.

"Here you go." Sliding the glasses onto the table, I dropped down beside Beth and sighed with relief. "Enjoy 'em because the next round is through the waitress." I wouldn't be making that mistake again.

Marjorie took a sip of hers and screwed her nose up in disgust. "Ew. You got me regular? I only drink diet."

"Sorry. I don't think you mentioned that."

"Well, duh." She shoved the glass aside and returned to a conversation she'd been having with Alex.

Duh. There went ten bucks and a half-hour of my life I'd never get back. And I couldn't even get a thank you?

"Sorry." Beth accepted her drink and took a large gulp. "She's not usually like that. She's just drunk."

"Mmhmm."I cracked my water bottle and downed nearly half of it in one swallow. The temperature may have taken a nosedive outside, but in that mob scene it was scorching.

"So, how do you think you did on the test?"

"Okay." I'd failed. There wasn't a doubt in my mind that no matter what I did for the remainder of the year, my grade for the course was beyond saving. I wasn't even sure if I'd keep attending. But that was not a conversation I wanted to have. "How about you?"

"Good. I think I did pretty well. The study group really helped, don't you think? We should do it again for the final."

I wouldn't know. Of the handful of sessions I'd actually attended, I'd managed to pay attention about a quarter of the time. "Sure. Definitely."

Ice cubes clinked against the side of her glass as she stirred them with her tiny red straw. "Maybe we could—"

"*Hey!* What do you think you're doing talkin' to *my* girl?" Tom grabbed Alex's shoulder and wheeled him around, nearly toppling him from his chair.

"I wasn't—"

Tom growled and Alex, not being a fool, threw his hands up in surrender. "Whatever, man. She's all yours."

Continuing to prove himself smarter than ninety percent of the bar's patrons, Alex got the hell out of Tom's way. Which, unfortunately left no buffer between him and Marjorie, who did not looked pleased to see him.

"What the hell is your problem, Tom?"

"*You!* Talking up other guys right in front of me like that. Playing stupid friggin' games. Are you *trying* to make me jealous? Because it won't work. I'd have to actually give a damn about your ass to be jealous, stupid bitch."

Marjorie's eyes flashed. "Screw you, Tom."

"You'd like that wouldn't you? I bet you'd just love to screw me right here on this table in front of everyone. And him." Tom thrust an angry finger in Alex's direction. "And him." That same finger swung toward me and I felt my skin prickle. "And every other guy in this place, you little slu—"

"*Enough!*" I was on my feet and in Tom's ugly face before the foul word could pass what was about to be a fat lip. "Why don't you watch your mouth?"

"Why don't *you* mind your own damn business?"

"You made it my business when you decided to turn a private matter into a spectacle for the whole damn table." Sometime during my intervention Marjorie cleared out and disappeared into the crowd.

Tom reached for his beer bottle and I shoved it away, not sure if he intended to use it for a drink or as a weapon. "I think you've had enough."

Tom was tall and worked hard to look scary, but I was bigger and I knew, if it came down to it, I could kick his scrawny ass. "You should go. Now."

ANGEL

Words didn't seem to be having much of an effect on him, but my hand planted in his shoulder did the trick. He stumbled backward and grabbed ahold of the table. I waited while Tom decided if he wanted to make this into something more, but he must have had at least a few brain cells still in operation because he turned, scooping up a stray shot and downed it on his way to the door. I just hoped he wasn't dumb enough to get behind the wheel.

"Stupid ass." My arms felt sore from how tightly flexed my muscles still were when I reclaimed my seat. I almost wished he had made it into something. I could have used the release.

Beth's eyebrows were practically at her hairline. "Caulder, relax. He didn't mean it. He's just—"

"Drunk? I'm getting really sick of listening to people use that as an excuse to act like assholes. Drunk is not an irreversible or unavoidable condition. Drunk is a *choice*. Just like how you *choose* to treat other people."

"You're right. It is. But I'm sure he didn't mean it. When he sobers up he'll feel bad. He'll apologize and—"

"Words cause more damage than they can heal. A simple 'I'm sorry' is not going to put back all the pieces they can break a person into."

Beth stared at me as if I'd grown a third head. "Caulder, I don't think Marjorie's going to break over this. Truthfully," she took a quick peek at her friend who was tearing it up on the dance floor with Alex and two other guys, and a slight smile tipped her lips, "I'm not even sure she's going to remember."

Shit. She was right. Marjorie was hardly some defenseless girl that needed my protection. In fact, I wasn't sure Tom's assessment of her character flaws was entirely off target. I'd overreacted.

"Sorry. I don't know what I was thinking." *Bullshit.* I knew exactly what—or *who*— I'd been thinking about. And it wasn't Beth, or Marjorie, or even dickhead Tom who needed to be on the receiving end of my long overdue lecture. "It's been a long day."

"It's okay." Beth nodded me straight off the hook, though it was nothing more than another lame excuse to act like an ass. "It's kinda sweet that you'd stand up for her like that."

ANGEL

"Yeah, well, I doubt Tom would agree. I think I'm gonna call it a night." I felt the beginnings of a headache taking root, and if I stayed there any longer, my head might actually explode. "You want a ride home?"

"Uh . . ." Her dark chocolate eyes slid past me again to where all of her friends were acting wild and crazy, and having a blast. Where she should be, celebrating her achievements, instead of trapped at the table with me and all of my crap.

"You stay. Have fun. Just promise me you'll call a cab later."

"Promise. But I wish you'd stay."

"Maybe next time."

With a smile and a gentle squeeze of my shoulder, Beth slid out of her seat and scooted past me into the melee to join the others. In the center of the chaos, they threw their hands up in the air and swayed to the music. They laughed and jumped and smiled. They had *fun*.

I felt like an interloper, watching from the table in the shadowed corner. As though I watched through glass, something I wanted, but couldn't quite touch. The only thing standing in my way was myself, but I knew . . . Even if I went out there and went through all the motions, I'd never find what I was looking for. It was buried too deep, beneath all of the other garbage inside of me.

I wasn't sure I'd ever find it again.

ANGEL

Twelve

Groaning into my pillow, I rolled over and slapped at the clock on my bedside table. Would I ever get a good night's sleep again? I'd laid awake for hours before exhaustion finally pulled me under and I was nowhere near ready to get up again. My fumbling fingers sought out the snooze button, stabbing at it repeatedly, but the noise refused to stop.

"What the—?"

Lifting my head, I blinked at the clock. And blinked again. 12:47? What the hell was my clock going off at nearly one in the morning for? Only it wasn't my clock. It was my cell phone . . . And it was ringing . . . At nearly one in the morning.

Shaking my sleep muddled brain into gear, I snatched it up and slid my finger across the smooth glass screen. My heart pounded against my ribs, knowing who it was, knowing something was wrong, before her soft voice ever hit my ears.

"Jade? What's wrong?"

"I . . . can't . . ." She gasped and choked on her words, sending my own lung function into overdrive.

"What? What happened?" No response, only more tiny gasps and a frightened whimper. "You can't *what*, Jade?"

"Breathe." The word was barely audible, but it's what I'd been expecting, so I heard it loud and clear.

"Okay." Easing off the bed, I aimed to keep my voice calm. Her desperate, stuttering breaths were scaring the crap out of me, but she was in the midst of a panic attack and if I added to that fear it would only make things worse. "Slow and steady." I pulled the phone away from my ear long enough to tug on a shirt from the foot of my bed. "Inhale . . . Exhale . . . Just breathe." She was trying. I could hear her trying to calm herself, but I knew firsthand how hard that could be. How painful. Panic attacks could make you feel like your lungs had sealed up. Set your whole chest on fire. "I know it hurts. Just breathe through it, Jade. Are you at home?"

"Yes." The terror filled word tore through me and I clenched my phone hard enough to make my bones ache.

"Is anyone there with you?" She didn't have much of a support system, I knew that, but she wasn't going to be able to break through the attack alone.

"My-my mother's . . . passed . . . out."

Goddammmit. There were a host of things I would have liked to call that pathetic excuse for a human being who had the nerve to call herself a parent, but it wasn't the time. Panic attacks weren't nearly as life threatening as they felt while having one. Worst case scenario she'd pass out from lack of oxygen and start breathing normally again on her own. But it was so much worse than that. She was upset, hurting, in agony, and all alone. I knew what that felt like and I'd be damned if I'd let her face it on her own.

"I'm on my way. Just keep breathing. I'm on my way."

It's entirely possible that I broke just about every traffic law known to mankind and set a new land speed record on my way to her apartment. The thought of her in pain, needing me, plagued my mind, adding lead to my foot.

I knew which building was hers and had since wrangled her apartment number out of Kiernan. If he wondered why I wanted to know, he hadn't asked. I flew up three flights of stairs, ignoring the rickety banister and dangerously sagging steps that otherwise would have aggravated me to no end.

Knocking, without really expecting an answer, I got none. Much to my simultaneous relief and distress, I found the door unlocked. Something else to worry about later.

"Jade?" I stepped inside, scanning the cluttered living room and froze when my eyes landed on the scene in the corner. Blood and glass covered the floor, streaks of it smearing down the hallway. "Jade, where the hell are you?"

I followed the gory trail to a hollow wooden door that stood open in a cracked frame.

For one eternally torturous moment, I thought I was too late. Blood streaked her face and hair, and she lay unmoving, clutching her chest on a small cot-like bed, which occupied nearly half the tiny room. When her eyes fluttered open, I sucked in a lungful of air I hadn't realized I needed. I even welcomed the fear and pain shining through them.

"Hey. Hey, it's okay." In two strides, I stood beside the bed and knelt to scoop her from the flimsy mattress. I honestly couldn't say if having her in my arms did more to sooth her or me, but I couldn't *not* hold her. She was so light, so disturbingly thin, cradling her small body like a child's was easy. Carefully, I lowered us both onto the bed so that she was settled in my lap and eased her head to my chest. "You're okay."

"I think . . . I'm having . . . a h-heart attack." She trembled in my arms and I held her closer, knowing that fear, knowing how it added to the terror and thus the pain in a vicious, endless cycle.

The first time I'd experienced a panic attack like that wasn't long after Kiernan had been diagnosed. It lasted over an hour and I was convinced I was going to die. The pain was almost unbearable, but the fear and the loneliness . . . those were worse. I never told anyone and it wasn't the last time it happened. But each time they became easier to recognize and control.

"You're not having a heart attack." The key to overcoming panic was to relax. My hand drifted up and down her rigid spine, seeking to ease some of the brittle tension from her body. "I know it feels that way, but you're alright. It's just a panic attack. It's completely normal. Just breathe. Breathe for me. Put your hand on my chest."

If I could get her breathing under control, the rest would follow. She continued to shake uncontrollably as her tiny hand lifted and flopped limply against my chest. It took all of my concentration to keep my breathing slow and steady beneath the warmth of her gentle touch, and I could only pray she wouldn't notice the frantic rhythm my heart had fallen into.

"There you go. Now concentrate on my breathing." Inhale. Hold. Exhale. Repeat. "You do it. Copy me. Just like me, Jade. In." I took a deep breathe, filling my lungs to capacity and drawing in the sweet scent of her hair. "And out." All of that air escaped in a silent gasp as I fought for control. "Keep going. In."

Intentionally shifting my face away from her, I continued the age-old cycle until I felt her falling into a similar, steady pattern and the tension began to ease from her body.

ANGEL

"There you go. That's better."

Her body slumped heavily against mine, weak from fatigue and the lingering effects of the panic.

"How did you know?" Her voice was a frail thread of sound.

"That it was a panic attack?" She nodded, not bothering to lift her head from where it rested directly above my heart, her soft hair brushing against the underside of my chin and throat, and I spit out the truth—something I'd never told anyone—without a second thought. "I've had one or two myself."

"And someone talked you through them?"

"Not exactly." With one problem under control, it was time to concentrate on another. "Now, where are you hurt?"

She sat up slowly, the look in her eyes telling me she had no clue what I was talking about. Was it possible she didn't even know she was injured?

"There's blood all over your face and in your hair, Angel. Where'd it come from?"

Confusion clouded her gaze and concern about a possible head wound started to creep in until her eyes widened in sudden realization and she gingerly peeled open her hands, baring tattered, bloody palms. Slivers of glass like I'd seen in the living room were still embedded in the torn flesh. Her face fell as whatever led up to the panic attack came crashing back and I felt her pain as though it were my own.

"Jade . . ." More than anything I wanted to take that pain away, draw it in, give it a place to grow and fester, and erase it from her life. But I couldn't. That pain was hers to bear and there wasn't a thing I could do about it.

"I didn't mean to."

"I know." There was another pain I *could* do something about, though. "Come on, let's get you cleaned up."

Jade stumbled twice in the less than twenty feet between her bed and the bathroom across the hall and it took every last ounce of my self-control not to reach out and steady her. The mirror above the sink housed three poorly supplied shelves, which I scanned as she plunked down on the toilet lid. A few outdated prescription bottles, a half used tube of toothpaste, two toothbrushes, a comb, and a handful of little black pins. Not much to work with.

"Do you have any gauze?"

"Actually, I think we do." She tipped her head sideways as tiny thought lines creased the skin at the top of her nose. "Try the top drawer under the sink."

I had to shimmy the thing just to get it open and when I did it was littered with an array of random crap, everything from loose pills that looked like aspirin to yellowing Q-tips. In the corner sat a small roll of unsealed gauze that looked anything but sanitary.

I did manage to dig out a pair of tweezers from the mess and located a pale blue washcloth in the narrow closet beside the shower. Not exactly the supplies I would have liked to have at my disposal, but they'd do.

Her hands were a mess and given the disaster area in the living room, I could only imagine how they'd gotten that way. I was no stranger to stupid, self-destructive behavior myself, but watching the blood ooze from the open wounds in her palms made me angry. I wanted to yell at her for being irresponsible enough to cause herself that kind of pain. But that would have made me a hypocritical ass and it definitely wasn't what she needed from me.

"I didn't see any peroxide."

"Huh?"

"In your cabinet. Do you have any?" Picking the last of the glass from her skin, I was relieved to see that at least the cuts all seemed to be superficial.

"Peroxide?"

"It's an antiseptic."

"We don't have anything like that."

Of course they didn't. "Then we're going to have to clean them up as best we can and keep them covered. You don't want to get an infection."

Letting the water run warm before I wet the washcloth and wrung it dry, I focused on tuning Jade out. This was going to sting like a bitch and I couldn't handle the thought of being the one to cause her pain. For her part, she stayed still and made very little noise while I cleaned and bandaged her hands.

"They don't look too deep. You shouldn't need stitches, but keep this on and rewrap them every morning." I hesitated to go any further, knowing it was none of my business. And knowing I wouldn't rest until I had an answer. "So how'd you do this to yourself, anyway?"

Jade ducked her head, allowing a waterfall of dark, silky hair to conceal the crimson blush creeping into her cheeks. "Got in a fight with a clock."

She acted like that was something to be ashamed of when anger was a perfectly natural response to the kind of situation she'd been thrown into.

"I put my fist through a wall. Not quite as symbolic, but it did the trick." Sometimes the pressure could get to be too damn much inside. Sometimes you had to find a way to let some of that pain out or you'd feel like you'd explode. Jade peeked at me through the curtain of hair, a sad hope glowing in her eyes that maybe she wasn't alone in feeling that way. "Mom was pissed. Yelled at me the whole way to the hospital and the entire time we sat in the waiting room. I kept waiting for her to lose her voice."

She never did. At the time I hadn't been particularly receptive to her outburst, but now it made me smile. It was just a broken hand, but she acted like I'd thrown myself into the path of an oncoming train. I was bigger and stronger than her, and yet she still felt the need to protect me. Even from myself. It's one of the reasons I loved her so fiercely. The kind of love she taught me. The kind she showed me my entire life. And looking at where I was, knowing Jade's mother slept right down the hall, while her daughter cried and bled and broke . . . It was one of the reasons I knew how damn lucky I was.

Following my train of thought around to the girl in front of me, I found her smiling back at me. And it took my breath away. The girl was beautiful—inside and out—I'd known that for a while, but when she smiled . . .

"Thanks, Cal." She pushed off the toilet and her smile instantly tightened into a pained grimace.

"I saw that. Where else are you hurt?"

She didn't even bother trying to lie, plopping back down on the toilet lid and lifting her feet from the water stained floor.

Tucking away my temper, I sighed and settled back on my heels. "You don't do anything halfway, do you?"

ANGEL

I had to wipe away the blood to be certain, but there didn't appear to be any glass embedded in these wounds. Not an easy task. She wiggled and squirmed, twisting her feet out of my grasp repeatedly, while she attempted to control herself and her laughter.

"Hold still." I gripped her ankle tighter, paying particular attention to the curve of her foot where she seemed to be the most ticklish. It may have been cruel and unusual, but it was all in the name of health. Plus, I would have done just about anything to hear her laugh a little while longer. "They don't look too bad. I'm gonna wrap them up just to keep the blood off your sheets for tonight, but by morning they should be alright. Maybe just wear a second pair of socks for some extra cushioning. And don't go running any marathons."

I finished wrapping her feet and lifted her before she could stand and do herself any more damage. Her body stiffened almost immediately, but if she thought I was going to let her walk on those raw feet now that I'd seen what they looked like, she had another thing coming.

Lying her in her bed and tucking her in probably wouldn't be found in any medical textbook, but it felt like the right thing to do. Sort of how leaving felt like the *wrong* thing to do. So I planted myself on the edge of her mattress and searched for an excuse to stay.

It was Jade who gave me one. "I'm sorry for dragging you out in the middle of the night. *Again*. And for blubbering all over you. *Again*."

She was apologizing . . . *Again*. It seemed like all that girl ever did was apologize. Like her existence was some kind of inconvenience to everyone around her. The thought that there were people in her life that would intentionally make her feel that way . . . "Don't ever apologize for your pain, Angel. It means you care. That you have a heart. Otherwise it couldn't break like this."

"Why do you keep calling me that?"

"Angel?" I'd thought of her that way since the moment I'd laid eyes on her. She was Angel to me before she was Jade. But I had no idea when I'd made the conscious decision to start calling her it out loud. Or if I even *had* made a conscious decision to do so. "Because you are one."

"What?" She looked at me like I was crazy and finally my temper broke through.

"I mean it. Look at you. Nothing about this is easy." How could she not see what an amazing person she was? What a difference she had made in Kiernan's life—and mine—at a severe cost to herself? "As far as I can see, nothing about your life is easy, at all. And yet here you are. I know Kiernan didn't want to hurt you, but I think a lot of the reason he didn't tell you sooner was because he didn't want to *lose* you."

"But, I'd never—"

"He knows that . . . *now*. But a lot of girls would have. Hell, his own father did. Can you really blame him for worrying about it?"

Her sleepy eyes struggled to stay open as she shook her head, nuzzling deeper into her pillow.

"I should get going. You hanging in there?"

"Yeah. Thank you, Cal. For everything."

Dark hair spilled across the pillowcase and over her shoulder, framing her delicately featured face. Tiny nose, slender chin, and sooty lashes fanned against her high cheekbones.

Sweet. Everything about this girl screamed sweet.

My gaze continued south to her bandaged hands clutching the blanket and a knot lodged in my throat.

Sweet and damaged.

"Good night, Angel." I shouldn't have done it. I knew I shouldn't do it when I did. But I couldn't keep myself from pressing my lips to her forehead. As though I could somehow kiss away all of her pain.

If only life were that simple.

Her breaths turned deep and even before I left the room. Down the hall, the living room greeted me with the same gruesome scene I'd found when I arrived. Not something I gathered her mother would appreciate. Or give a damn about. And not something Jade should have to deal with in the morning.

Rooting through cabinets made me want to hit something. The ones in the kitchen were barer than the ones in the bathroom. No wonder she was so thin.

I did manage to come away with some paper towels and a bottle of store brand cleaning solution from under the sink, a broom, and cracked dust pan. After sweeping up the shattered debris, I dumped the destroyed timepiece in the trash and set to scrubbing some of the stains from the worn carpet.

ANGEL

On hands and knees in some woman's living room I'd never met—but already despised— after two in the morning. My life was becoming all sorts of complicated.

Thirteen

Male bonding: where two or more men gather to maim, kill, and otherwise obliterate . . . pretty much anything. Or experience all of the above vicariously through the big screen at the Cineplex. In IMAX 3D. By the time Kiernan and I hit the lobby, I was pretty sure I was deaf in at least one ear. Totally worth it.

"That was awesome." Kiernan pitched his empty popcorn bucket in the trashcan, headed for the door. "Thanks for coming."

"You know me . . . Any excuse to watch shit go boom, count me in."

Kiernan grinned and threw open the glass door, stepping into the sunlight. It was a beautiful day for late November and I forced myself to relax. Even good days could get to be too much. As hard as I tried to enjoy the good times while they were happening, there was always that voice in the back of my head wondering how many more good times I'd get. If this could possibly be the last one. For the moment, I told that voice to 'stuff it' and trailed Kiernan out to where he'd parked.

Kiernan drove. He almost always drove because he liked to drive. Personally, I couldn't have cared less. Back in California, I loved cruising in my baby, showing her off with the sun gleaming off a fresh wax job. But here, I didn't really have anyone to show her off *to*. And sunshine was something dreams were made of.

Fall was breathtaking in the northeast. For all of about forty-eight hours. Then all of those brilliantly colored leaves seemed to rip themselves from their life-giving source and plummet to the earth at once. Couldn't blame them, knowing what came next. Rain, snow, sleet. Unsavory combinations of the three. The ground was always wet, the sky was always gray, and I was bordering on a serious vitamin D deficiency. The blue skies and bright sun above us were a rare gift from the gods. One I fully intended to soak up for as long as possible.

We were almost home when the music cut out, announcing an incoming call from Jade.

Kiernan smiled and hit a button on the steering wheel. "Hey. Are you at my place? We're on our way back. We should be there in—"

"No, Kiernan. I'm not at your place." Jade's voice was ripe with anxiety.

"Oh. Okay, are you home? Do you want me to come pick you up?" Kiernan shifted his hands on the wheel, tightening his grip as I leaned almost unconsciously closer to the speaker.

"Yeah. I'm at home . . . with your mom."

When she paused, my entire body tensed, waiting for her to continue. I don't know what I expected. Something about that dirtbag neighbor of hers? Her mother? Maybe. But *our* mother? The thought never crossed my mind.

I opened my mouth to respond, but Kiernan waved me off. "My mom?"

"Ask her what she's doing there." Kiernan glared at me and I shrugged. He was the one who took the call on speaker.

"What's my mom doing there?"

ANGEL

"I don't—" Jade's voice cracked and it hit me like a punch to the gut. Whatever this was, it was bad. And it involved not only my Angel, but my mom.

"Turn the car around." I pointed out a dirt side road where Kiernan could pull a uey, hell bent on getting to them as quickly as possible.

"Talking to my mom. She wants you to come and get me." Why was I not surprised that Jade's mother was involved? I liked to consider myself a pretty laid back person when it came to getting along with others. There weren't many people I didn't like. But I *hated* that woman.

"We're on our way." The tires kicked up dirt as Kiernan cut the wheel, turning us back toward Halfmoon Park. "Meet me outside. I'll be there in five."

My foot pressed against a phantom gas pedal the entire way, silently urging Kiernan to drive faster than Great Aunt Bessy. When we rolled up in front of her building, Jade was standing there, arms wrapped protectively around her narrow waist. Kiernan was at her side almost before he had the car in park.

I took a minute to check my emotions. Jade was finally starting to let her shield down around me. Last night she'd allowed me a glimpse behind the curtain of composure she wore like a second skin. The last thing I needed to do was let my anger get the better of me and frighten her. Send those walls shooting right back up. How was I supposed to help her deal with what she was going through if I couldn't even see it?

"What's going on up there?" Jade twisted around to face me as I joined them on the sidewalk.

"I don't know." Guilt shone bright through her glassy eyes. "Your mom told me to leave."

And there went that lip back between her teeth again.

"Should I—?" I tipped my head toward the building, uncertain how Jade would react to my offer.

"No!" The bug-eyed dread was more than I expected. "She said they needed to talk, privately."

I called bullshit. This was about more than my mother's wishes. Jade was genuinely distressed at the thought of me going in there. At my mother being in there. Alone.

And so was I.

ANGEL

"No offense, Angel, but I don't really feel comfortable leaving her alone up there with your mom."

Jade shuffled her feet over the cracked concrete. "She may be . . . *vocal* every now and then, but she's in no shape to hurt anyone physically."

Despite all of the awful things he'd told me about her mother, Kiernan nodded his agreement. "It's true. And you know Mom can handle the rest." His attempt to smile at Jade was pathetic. Kiernan hadn't developed the same kind of shield she and I had. He hadn't had a reason to. For that I was grateful. *Usually.* "Working in the ICU comes with the added bonus of developing a thick skin. You should hear some of the crap nurses have to listen to."

While I listened to my brother try to ease Jade's remorse, my gaze drifted back to the building and up to the third floor. I wasn't usually one to take other people's word for it. I liked to see things for myself. Maybe I had trust issues, I don't know. But that look on Jade's face, and the fact that I really *did* trust her was enough to still my restless feet.

"Let's go." Kiernan steered Jade toward the car. "Mom wanted her out of here, we're getting her out of here. She'll be fine, Cal."

***

The one universal pitfall of all teenaged guy's dream cars was the serious lack of backseat leg room. Who the hell cares how much space is between one seat and the next as long as it can go from zero to one-twenty in two-point-five?

The guy who's stuck back there eating his knees, that's who.

Leaving the complex behind didn't calm Jade down. If anything her anxiety only seemed to ratchet up a few more notches. She was edging dangerously close to another panic attack. If she couldn't relax . . .

Without thinking, I reached for her small shoulders. Maybe I could help rub away—

Kiernan's hand settled on her knee and I froze, hands hovering awkwardly over the top of the seat. What the hell was I thinking? She *had* someone to help ease her worry. And it was most certainly *not* me.

ANGEL

Doing my best not to be a complete voyeur, I tried to imagine what a conversation between my mother and Jade's mother would be like. It wasn't pretty. Mom was a good person. Kind, understanding, passionate. It was that last one that could get her into trouble. She was very passionate when it came to things she cared about. And Jade was one of those things.

It was easy to see why Jade had won a place in her heart, but that probably meant bad things for Jade's mother. And Jade's mother didn't seem the type to take bad things lying down. In fact, she seemed the type to take those bad things, turn around, and dump them all over someone else—namely *Jade*. When Mom was in a mood, Kiernan and I knew well enough to stay out of her way. She didn't come looking for us and she'd never intentionally take it out on us. Jade wasn't so lucky. Odds were, by the time she got home, her mom would be looking to unload a lot of crap. And in that tiny apartment, there was nowhere for her to hide.

There was a lot of shit in her life that scared her, but this did not have to be one of those things. "If our mom stirs up trouble, I'm sure she won't mind you crashing at our house for a few days until things settle down."

And that had absolutely nothing to do with me wanting her where I could keep an eye on her.

"No." The thought seemed to horrify her, which—I won't lie—I took a little personally.

Despite Kiernan's additional urging, she steadfastly refused to stay away from that hell-hole any longer than strictly necessary. A response I truly could not understand. She was obviously terrified of the idea of going back to face her mother, and yet she refused to accept a pardon, intent on doing exactly that.

We wrestled our way through the front door like a pack of wild animals, desperate to escape the whipping wind and biting cold. The sun had disappeared behind the ever-present bundle of clouds, taking any hope of warmth right along with it. Frigid was too kind of a word to describe the weather here. Obscene was more like it, and it wasn't even technically winter yet.

My thick winter coat felt heavy folded over my arm as I stood back, watching Kiernan hang Jade's sorry excuse for a jacket in the hall closet. Thin blooded or not, just looking at that thing made me shiver.

"What happened to your hands?"

ANGEL

I ignored Kiernan's outburst, groping in the closet for a hanger of my own, but listened carefully for Jade's response. I'd been wondering since yesterday if she'd tell him about what happened, about calling me. It was the kind of thing I usually tried to shield my brother from, but would she do the same? *Could* she?

"Nothing. The stupid clock on my living room wall fell last night and I cut my hands trying to clean it up." The lie tumbled smoothly from her lips, matching perfectly that mask she wore so well.

I loathed it.

And then I donned my own.

"Are you okay?" Kiernan peeled back her bandage, peeking underneath. Something I desperately wanted to do myself. "Are you sure you don't need stitches? Mom could—"

"No. I'm fine, Kiernan. Really. She already looked. They're not even bleeding anymore. I just didn't want them to get infected."

Knowing Mom had taken a look eased some of the residual worry that had been plaguing me since I left her with little more than a washcloth and a Band-Aid. Not nearly the kind of care I wanted her to have.

Growing up with only a brother, I didn't know much about entertaining girls. I mean, I knew how to entertain a *girlfriend*, no problem, but not so much a girl *friend*. Jade had retreated inside her own head and was thinking entirely too much. Whatever was happening back at her place, there wasn't anything we could do about it now. And whatever was coming next couldn't be dealt with until we got there. So, for the meantime, it was probably best to get her mind on something else. *Anything* else.

As a last resort, I raided the DVD cabinet, grudgingly moving into my mother's section. I swear the word 'love' was in more than half the titles and every cover looked like a slight variation of the one before it. How did she even tell these things apart? Choosing one at random, I popped it in the Blu-ray player and we all settled on the couch.

It seemed to work. For a while. But as soon as those credits rolled, I could tell we were losing her again. Convinced I wouldn't survive another chic-flick, I went with plan B.

Kiernan wasn't thrilled when I pulled out the old family albums. We hadn't looked at them in years. After the move, I'd been the one to unpack them and I'd intentionally hidden them at the back of the bookcase. Too many memories. But now seemed like as good a time as any to revisit them.

We'd been so many places, seen so many things. In some ways it proved that Kiernan had gotten a lot out of his seventeen years. In others, it served to remind us of everything he'd be leaving behind. Bittersweet emotions clouded every page, every story.

Dad was in almost all of the pictures. Mom was the family photographer, so she was in a group shot here and there. A few candid shots. But Dad was in nearly every single one. He was such a huge part of our lives. He was my goddamn hero. Nothing in my eighteen years with the man had led me to believe he was a spineless coward, but when he packed his shit, claiming 'he couldn't deal' after Kiernan's diagnosis, he proved himself to be exactly that. It felt like a giant chunk was carved from me. For a long time, I didn't know who I was without him. I was Caulder Parks, son of Sam Parks, future CEO of *Parks Steiner, LLC.*

That's who I was. Always.

Until I wasn't.

By unspoken agreement, Kiernan and I ignored his presence and managed to find a way to share our many misadventures with Jade without mentioning him once. For me, it was anger that excluded him from our lives. For Kiernan, it was guilt. He denied it, but I knew deep down he still blamed himself for Dad leaving. Which only made me madder.

Jade's fingernails were bitten almost all the way to the quick. I suppressed a cringe at the tender exposed skin, knowing how painful that could be. It was a habit I'd picked up as a kid. One I'd thankfully broken. Her slender fingers traced over each individual image, studying them, committing them to memory. I was happy to share them with her, but it saddened me to know that she had few—if any—happy memories of her own. Had she ever gone rock climbing? Horseback riding? Had she ever seen the ocean? Did she have a single photo where she stood side-by-side with her family and smiled? Somehow, I doubted it.

Before she reached the final shot, Kiernan snatched the album from her grasp and slid it closer to himself. I took a second peek at the page, curious about what it was that caught his attention. It wasn't a particularly interesting set of photos. One of the two of us body surfing off the coast of Mexico, a couple pretty landscapes that Mom must have liked, and a family shot. Mom and Dad—arms around each other—Kiernan and me in front. Happy, smiling faces. A family with no clue that their entire world was about to be blown apart.

Kiernan skimmed the tip of his finger along the outline of the photo, but I doubted he was really seeing it. His gaze had turned inward, eyes glassy. A cold lump solidified in the pit of my stomach. I'd seen that look before.

"Where's my mom?" He looked to Jade for an answer and she startled slightly beside him.

And why shouldn't she? It appeared this particularly *fun* side of Kiernan's condition was all new to her. "With . . . my mom?"

"Oh." Kiernan's gaze dropped back to the picture and his thumb stroked over Dad's smiling face. This wasn't going to end well. "And my dad? Where's he? Still at work?"

Shit. Jade looked completely lost. So did Kiernan. I was the only one in the room who had any freaking clue what the hell was going on. And I wished I didn't.

"Would you excuse us for a minute, Jade? I need to speak with my brother." I tried to act normal. Like the awkward level hadn't just hit the roof.

Jade wasn't the type of girl who couldn't take a hint. She cleared out quick and quiet, with only a passing glance in my direction that let me know exactly how freaked out she really was. Kiernan sat watching her go and I wondered if he even knew who she was. Tumors did funny things to memories, mixed them up, erased them, muddled them. I couldn't imagine how frustrating that must have been at times.

"Kiernan?"

"Where's Dad?" There was a bite to his words. Being confused was one thing, but he *knew* he was confused. He *knew* there was something he should remember. He just couldn't. And it pissed him off.

"He's gone."

"Gone where?"

It wasn't the first time we'd had this conversation. It wasn't even the second. But it never hurt any less. "He left, Kier. After your diagnosis. He packed his shit and bailed. Before we moved back here. Remember?"

ANGEL

Probably not the gentlest way to break it to him, but the doctors said that the more detail I provided, the easier it would be for him to latch onto the memory.

"He . . . left us?" Kiernan's brow scrunched and I watched his eyes flick side to side, searching his brain for the elusive knowledge.

It was bad enough that he had to go through this once in his life, but each time he forgot it was like losing Dad all over again for him. It sucked in a big, big way. Mom couldn't bring herself to talk about him—and I didn't want her to have to—so I got to play the bearer of bad news again and again.

Slowly understanding dawned on him. "Yeah. Right. I knew that."

"Of course you did."

"I just . . . I forgot. Sorry."

"Nothing to be sorry for." A slap on his shoulder drew him out of whatever residual memories lurked fresh and raw in his mind.

"Where's Jade?"

"She's in the kitchen."

"She saw . . .?" And there it was. The humiliation I'd been trying to avoid by sending her away. He was mortified.

"Kiernan, it's no big deal. You get a little confused sometimes, so what? It's not like it's your fault. She understands that. I'll explain it to her." He couldn't even bring himself to look at *me.* How was he going to face her? "It's *Jade* we're talking about, Kier. You really think she'd think any less of you because of this? What you two have . . . it's something special. *She's* something special. Don't let your pride get in the way of that."

It was easy to make statements like that being on the outside, looking in. Kiernan was a guy and guys have a thing about weakness. They have a special hatred for looking weak in front of their girl. Kiernan wasn't weak. He was the strongest person I knew. But he didn't see it that way. Not that it mattered. He wasn't even hearing me. Too lost in his own shame to listen to what I was saying.

"*Kiernan!*" His startled gaze flicked up to meet mine and I held it steady. "Do not let that damn tumor take any more from you than it already has. Let it go. Do you understand me?"

ANGEL

Embarrassment morphed into confusion, followed quickly by acceptance, and with it returned a bit of that fire I liked to see in his eyes. The fire that said he still had some fight left in him. And he planned to use every last ounce of it.

"You're right. Screw the tumor. I won't let it win. Not against her."

"Good." That's what I liked to hear. *Not today, bastard. You don't get to win today.* "I'm going to go find Jade. I'll be right back."

She was pacing like a caged lioness back and forth across the darkened kitchen. The sun was beginning to set outside and she hadn't even bothered to turn on a light, too lost in her own world of worry and fear to notice. A world she knew well. One she seemed to spend a majority of her time in. One I wished I could reach into and rescue her from. Except, where would I take her? I lived in that world, too.

Her pale skin glowed against the darker backdrop of her hair, fingers tangling in the long locks only to break free and tangle once more. The moment I stepped into the room, the lioness pounced.

"Is he okay? Is there something wrong with—?"

"He's fine." Wide, anxious eyes stared back at me, desperate to believe what I was telling her. "It's the tumor. Sometimes it puts a little extra pressure on his brain and makes him . . . confused."

"How long does it last?"

"Depends. Usually not long. He's fine now. Just embarrassed. He hates it when he forgets stuff like that. It's why I asked you to leave the room. It wasn't personal. He just . . . didn't need an audience."

"No. Of course not." It was good to see her stop and take a breath. She was learning as she went. Tossed into the deep end, without as much as a floaty. Scary things kept happening without warning, without explanation. The stress of that could be overwhelming at times. "That's awful."

"Yeah. It's not particularly fun having to hear that your dad bailed on you when you needed him most over and over again, and feeling like it's the first time, every time." I don't know what possessed me to lay that crap on her. She had a way about her that calmed me. Comforted me. Maybe I was getting *too* comfortable.

ANGEL

"It can't be much fun having to be the one to break the news over and over again, either."

I stopped breathing. A few words from her lips and it was like my lungs simply shut down and forgot how to function. Worse . . . I didn't even care.

I lived behind a wall. Hell, I *was* the damn wall. And I painted it with smiling faces and strong steel beams. But beneath all the fancy artwork, the wall was made of cardboard. She saw that. This broken girl, this battered Angel, saw beyond all the pretty pictures and false façade to what lie underneath.

Me. She saw *me*.

And that scared the crap out of me.

Fourteen

Sober.

Jade's mom was getting sober.

From what I understood, that was a first for her. Practically a damn miracle. But if the past year and a half had taught me anything, it was that miracles didn't exist. God? Heaven? I held out hope—mainly for Kiernan's sake—but I'd been disappointed too many times to have faith in miracles, anymore.

Maybe I was becoming a cynical mess. Maybe there was hope for her. For Jade. But I hated the idea of her suffering that kind of disappointment.

A loud buzz started up on my nightstand, followed by a single ear-piercing beep. I'd been lying in the same position for hours. The mattress, the pillow, all of it perfectly conformed to my body. I really didn't want to mess that up, so I groped aimlessly until my fingers closed around the cold plastic of my phone. Beth's name was scrawled across the top of the screen, followed by this message:

Hey. You awake?

What was the point of texting someone, setting off their phone—which was more than likely within arm's reach no matter what time of night it was—and asking if they're awake? If I wasn't before, I would have been now. Luckily, for her, sleep wasn't something I accomplished very easily. Or very often.

Yeah. What's up?

Are you going swimming in the morning?

I was planning to.

Mind if I drop by?

Did I mind? I thought I would have. Swimming was *my* time. The time that I had to myself, away from the constant stress and drama of my life. But having someone to share it with somehow felt less imposing than I expected it would.

Sure. Why not?

Great :) I'll see you at seven.

There's nothing worse than feeling like you're blind in one eye after ten minutes of staring at your bright phone screen in your darkened room with your face smooshed into a pillow and one eye shut to stabilize your depth perception. Except, maybe, actually *being* blind in one eye. And being blind in *both* probably wasn't great, either. And, yeah okay, there were a few things I could think of that were worse than that, too, but that's beside the point. Squeezing my eyes shut, I waited for my right pupil to dilate again so I could actually see, and considered what I'd just gotten myself into.

***

Tiny fractured particles of light danced and played on the smooth surface above me. I was weightless, floating. My mind, finally quieted, focused on nothing but my next breath, which I refused to take for as long as possible. For almost a full minute-and-a-half at a time . . . I was free.

Splash.

The particles moved into a frenzy and my peace was ruptured. Cool morning air wrapped around my shoulders and I surrendered to the urge to draw some into my lungs. Shaking the sopping hair from my face, I scanned the pool just in time to see Beth breaking the surface.

"Morning." She smiled and used her entire arm to swipe her long locks back over her shoulder. It floated around her in the water like threads of pure gold. The lights that I'd found so soothing abandoned me for her, dancing amongst the strands.

"Good morning."

"The water's nice." Her arms were fanned out beside her, slowly sweeping back and forth across the rippling surface. "What were you doing under there?"

"Breathing."

"What?" Beth laughed as though it were a joke, which must have been how it sounded to her, and I shook it off.

"Nothing. Never mind." I paddled in place and what I *thought* was a brilliant idea at the time occurred to me. "You wanna race?"

A smile broke over Beth's face. "Only if you're ready to lose."

"Oh-ho. Is that how it is?" I started backstroking toward the wall.

"That's how it is." She fell into a graceful butterfly stroke that I only knew the name of.

"Wait. Are you a swimmer?"

Her smile grew mischievous. "Captain of the varsity team in high school, baby."

Well . . . Damn. I was screwed. Swimming was a hobby of mine. A workout, maybe. I could do it, but I certainly wasn't going to be winning any awards.

"You ready? You look a little nervous? You can still back out if you don't want to get beat by a girl."

"No way. There's a first time for everything, right?"

"On your mark." She took hold of the wall with both hands, knees bent all the way to her stomach, feet planted against the side.

"Get set." I tried to copy her pose, but it was easier said than done. My body did not bend that way.

Beth flashed me one last, victorious smile. "Go!"

ANGEL

She took off like a rocket. I swear the girl was halfway across the pool before my brain even processed the command.

My height and long arms gave me an advantage and made it *almost* a fair race. She still beat me. By several lengths.

By the time I caught up to her, she was sitting on the edge of the pool with her feet dangling in the water, a huge grin on her face. I grabbed the wall and heaved myself out beside her, trying to catch my breath. Beth was even breathing hard.

"Alright, I can admit defeat. Even to a girl."

She laughed at my lame attempt at humor and glanced back out over the empty water. "You're a good swimmer. It's just your technique that could use some work."

"I spent a lot of time in the ocean. Technique was saved for other things." I realized how that sounded the minute it popped out of my mouth. Too late to do anything about it.

Luckily, Beth didn't seem to notice. "The ocean? Where are you from, Caulder? I don't really know anything about you. I could be swimming with an axe murderer."

There was a reason for that. The closer you got to people the more they wanted from you. And the more I wanted to give it to them. My plate was full, at the moment.

"Well, we're in a pool, so if I was a murderer, there would be more efficient means than an axe." Because that wasn't a totally creepy thing to say. "Originally, I'm from California."

Not exactly true. Technically, I was a local, *originally*. But after a decade, I liked to think of myself as a native Californian.

"California. Wow. So that's how you got so good at swimming."

Couldn't exactly grow up on the coast and *not* know how to swim. "How about you?"

"Oh about a zillion hours in the pool at home."

"You have a pool? Indoor?" Just a guess because I was pretty sure she was a local, too.

"Yup. It's great. Huge. I practically spent my entire life in that thing."

Our house was freaking ginormous. We had enough spare bedrooms to house a small army. And yet it lacked the one thing I'd probably get the most use out of. How the hell had that happened?

"But you don't swim for the college?" Who goes from captain of the varsity team to swimming morning races with me?

Beth shrugged. "It was fun while it lasted, but there isn't enough time to train anymore. I got accepted on an academic scholarship. Actually, I got both, but the academic one looks better on a resume, so I dropped the swimming and focused on studies. I have to maintain a three-point-seven GPA for the scholarship, but I'd really like to graduate summa cum laude."

"Wow." I was impressed. And a little intimidated. "That's . . . a lot."

"Yeah." She sighed, but it was a happy sigh. Beth was one of those people who thrived in chaos. Like me.

I wondered if things weren't the way they were if I'd be like her. Setting unrealistic goals just to struggle to meet them. Probably.

"You know one thing about swimming that never changes, no matter where you do it?" Beth stretched her arms out behind her and arched backward to shake out her hair.

It wasn't her hair that I was looking at, though. "Huh?"

"It always leaves me starving." She stood and snagged a pale pink towel from beside my pile of stuff. "Wanna grab some breakfast?"

Before I could open my mouth, my stomach decided to answer for me. The growl was loud enough to echo off the tile walls. "Sure. I could go for a bite."

"Great. I'm just going to change." She slipped into the girl's locker room.

Normally I didn't bother changing until I got home and could hop in the shower, but if she felt the need before we went wherever she had in mind, I probably should, too.

***

My skin felt itchy and tight from the chlorine. It was driving me crazy, trying not to scratch like a dog with fleas in the passenger seat of Beth's corvette. Not a classic, but its cherry red paint job and black ragtop still earned her a lot of envious stares. Some upbeat bubblegum pop station pumped through the speakers.

When we pulled up outside of a small restaurant and some ballad about the power of love snapped off mid verse, I couldn't have been happier. I didn't even care where we were.

"Table for two?" We followed a short girl around our age, maybe slightly older, past rows of empty booths to a small table tucked out of the way. "Can I get you anything to drink?"

"Coffee, please."

"Same for me." Beth took a seat across from me. Not that she had much of a choice. The tiny table only had two chairs.

"So . . ." Scratching the skin off my arms beneath the table, I sat back and glanced around the restaurant. "Nice place."

It seemed more like the type of place you'd go to for a fancy dinner. Low lighting, privacy walls between booths, unlit candles on every table alongside vases of some kind of small, white flowers. Their breakfast service didn't seem to draw quite as much interest. Beth and I were alone aside from a few servers, wandering around, filling sugar bowls and laying out utensils.

"Yeah. My family comes here for celebrations sometimes. But they make killer banana pancakes that aren't on the dinner menu."

"Guess I know what I'm ordering." I flashed her a grin and folded my menu. "So you live around here?"

"Yeah." She named a town I knew to be about a forty minute commute from school. "You, too, right? I mean, you're local, too?"

"Yeah. I live about a half hour from school. Only in the opposite direction." I have no idea why I didn't just tell her where I lived. It wasn't a secret. There was nothing to be ashamed of. We lived in a nice town. Or, at least, a nice *part* of town.

My mind went to the 'not so nice' parts of town and my thoughts took an unwelcome turn.

"Have you decided what you'd like to eat?" The waitress was back, delivering a much needed mug of sustenance.

We both ordered the banana pancakes before I was able to indulge in my first sip. I could literally *feel* my brain cells coming to life. My dramatic sigh brought Beth to laughter again. She laughed a lot. I liked that. There wasn't nearly enough laughter in my life.

"Fellow coffeeaholic like me, huh?" She took a sip of hers and groaned. "They make the best coffee, too."

"I have to admit it's pretty good. And I'm a bit of a coffee snob. Not easily impressed."

"Glad I picked a place that could live up to your high standards, then. Not like that cart sludge they serve on campus."

"Definitely not." I knew exactly what she was talking about. The coffee cart at school was fine in cases of emergency, but I definitely hadn't visited it the handful of times I'd caved for the taste.

"Here you are." Two plates of steaming pancakes slid onto the table between us and the chunks of real banana baked in set my mouth to watering. "Can I get you anything else?"

I turned down the offer of a refill and barely even noticed the waitress leaving. "This smells fantastic."

"Told ya so. Wait 'til you taste it." Beth cut off a chunk and shut her eyes as she slipped it past her lips.

I caught myself staring. Not that I could be blamed, but still . . . Refocusing on the equally delectable food in front of me, I took a bite of my own.

"Damn."

We lapsed into silence as we savored the sweet taste of bananas, walnuts, and maybe just a hint of vanilla? Whatever it was, it was incredible.

"So . . ." Beth straightened in her seat and twisted a finger in her hair. She was trying to look nervous, but she wasn't. Not really. I knew what nervous looked like and she never once broke eye contact. Beth had a ton of confidence. That could be a really attractive feature in a girl, but there was only one reason I could think of that she'd be pretending not to. "There's this concert Friday night at the theater downtown. I was wondering if maybe you'd—"

"Beth." *Dammit.* I'd had a feeling this was headed somewhere last night, but held to the hope that I was overthinking things, letting my ego get in the way. Evidently, my ego was just fine. "I'm sorry. I didn't mean to give you the wrong impression. I'm just . . . "

Just what? Shutting down a perfectly nice girl?

What was wrong with me? Beth was nice, and funny, and *hot*. We had a lot of similar interests. The girl was practically the female version of me, minus all the crap. But that was it.

That was the difference. The crap hadn't just affected my life, it had affected me. *Changed* me. Made me into who I was, for better or worse. Without that, I was . . . I didn't know who I was, anymore.

"I'm really busy right now. There's a lot of stuff that I'm dealing with and I just don't have the time for a relationship." Or the emotional fortitude.

The logic behind my decision was simple. Letting people in was done on a strict need basis. There were people I needed in my life. Beth wasn't one of them.

"It's okay." She smiled. Perfect, white teeth all lined up neatly between a pair of ruby red lips. Beth really was a beautiful girl, in the classic sense, but it took a lot more than a pretty face to impress me these days. "I get it. I'm really busy with school, too. The workload is crazy this year and it's only pre-med. Things are just going to get crazier from here."

"Yeah." I sank back in my chair and took another sip of coffee. "Crazy."

Fifteen

The countdown had begun. Only twelve shopping days left. Somewhere there were a dozen drummers drumming. And the 'spirit' had yet to hit me. In fact, this time of year had become a bit depressing. Not because of Kiernan. Or Dad. But because that little kid, nauseating, so excited you're going to puke feeling had disappeared. Overshadowed by reality, it just didn't hold the same magical fascination it once had. And that sucked.

Growing up sucked. I didn't like it. But who said you had to? Kiernan didn't have to. He was never even going to get the chance to. So how was it fair that he had to leave his childhood behind and yet never reach adulthood?

It wasn't.

ANGEL

And my four AM, seriously sleep deprived brain had a solution for that.

***

The boxes were all in the back of the attic, which was effing freezing. So much for heat rising. It was like the freaking arctic tundra up there. My toes grew numb while I sorted through mounds of shiny, glittery crap.

What about Christmas demands sparkles? Did it suddenly become some sort of fairy holiday I was unaware of? I was going to have to shower for a week straight to get it all out of my hair.

Looking a little like the jolly old elf, himself—with red nose and rosy cheeks—I hauled it all downstairs and set to work. It was a bigger project than I ever expected. Before dawn, I'd stabbed myself with more tacks than I cared to admit. Fingers wrapped in half-a-dozen Band-Aids, I cleared a path to the basement—and the fuse box—just in case. The two thousand extension cords it had taken me hours to connect and hide all coalesced through two separate surge protectors into one final plug I held in my hand. I was no electrician, but I didn't have high hopes as I shoved it into the socket in the foyer and held my breath.

No pops. No cracks. No spontaneous combustion. That was good.

Slowly, I twisted away from the wall and . . . *Wow*. Not to ring my own bell, but . . . Yeah. Damn. *Ding-a-ling*. Even I had to admit, the sparkles worked. Who knew I had a future in interior design? Maybe all of those hours I'd spent pouring over medical texts had been a waste.

Inhaling the invigorating scent of smooth, rich roasted beans, I indulged in a cautious sip of the scalding coffee. Black and hot, just the way I liked it. I could feel it burning a path all the way to my stomach, warming me from the inside out as I leaned against the counter and listened to Kiernan's footsteps coming down the stairs.

"*Wow*." He backed into the room, still surveying my hard work. "Mom went all out this year, didn't she?"

I was sure she would have if she'd had the time. With the upturn in nasty weather, the hospital had been overcrowded and understaffed for weeks. Mom was pulling double, sometimes triple, shifts for no other reason than to help out.

ANGEL

She was sleeping, eating, and showering there some days. I hadn't even seen her in twenty-four straight hours. As far as I was concerned, she deserved all the credit in the world. "Looks like."

"Where is she, now?"

"Back at the hospital."

"Like I needed to ask." Kiernan deposited a large white box on the counter and reached for the coffee pot.

"What's in the box?"

He only poured half a mug, and stopped to flip open the lid on his way to the fridge. Black boots with purple markings, fringed with white fur along the top sat nestled inside.

"Nice style. Can't wait to see what they look like on your feet."

"Shut up. They're for Jade. For Christmas." He dumped what looked to be about half a gallon of milk in his cup and turned to the sugar bowl.

"You got her *boots*?" I had to hold my gag reflex in check while I watched him shovel sweetener into his mug, mix it all up, and take a healthy gulp. That was *not* coffee. What he had in his cup was closer to a coffee flavored milkshake. What a waste.

"And a coat."

Oh, brother. He may have had his charms, but when it came to stuff like this, Kiernan was completely clueless. "How romantic."

"Stuff it. I wanted to get her a puppy, but I think her mom might have freaked. Besides, she needs a warm coat and you know she won't be getting one anywhere else."

He had a point. His gifts were practical and sorely needed. Jade was the type of girl to appreciate that. But she was still a girl. And deep down, every girl wants something pretty.

***

Playing super secret spy on Kiernan and Jade hadn't been my plan. It just sorta . . . happened. I was sitting on the couch, flipping through the pages of a sci-fi novel I'd picked up at the library during my last 'research' run. It was good, but with the amount of homework the professors kept heaping on, it was difficult to find time for pleasure reading.

I heard them come through the door and sank lower—concealing myself from view—for reasons I blame wholly on my ego. I wanted to experience her reaction, unhampered by my presence. I wanted Jade, real and unguarded. The way she only ever seemed to be around my brother.

"It's amazing." I couldn't see her face clearly from my position, but the wistful quality of her voice brought a smile to mine.

And then . . . she laughed. A sound so beautiful I wished I could record it and play it back whenever I needed to hear it.

Hello, ego, welcome to the surface.

I wasn't the only one who enjoyed it. "I love the sound of your laugh. I don't hear it nearly enough."

I grinned, listening to her sputter at Kiernan's praise until the phone rang and he left to take the call.

It had been nine days since I'd laid eyes on her. Nine precarious days without hearing her voice or having the slightest clue how things were going for her and her mother. Kiernan spoke with her every day by phone—sometimes several times a day—but I hadn't heard from her, at all. I didn't know how to take that. Whether things were going as smoothly as Kiernan seemed to believe, or if she was putting on a show for him and avoiding me, knowing I'd see straight through the bullshit. It was that second thought that kept me up at night.

I couldn't take it any longer. I *had* to know.

"He's right, you know." I shoved up high enough to see her over the arm of the couch and watched as she nearly tripped over her feet in surprise. There was a moment of panic where I knew I'd never reach her in time if she went down, but it settled when she regained her balance. "You don't laugh enough."

When I looked at her, I didn't see shields. I saw Jade. A crimson flush creeping into her cheeks. She looked so . . . angelic. Like *she* should be sitting on top of our Christmas tree. I wanted to ask her how things were going. If her mother was doing alright. If she was alright. But I could hear Kiernan wrapping up the call in the kitchen.

She looked okay. Better than okay. She looked *happy*. A new look for her. One that I liked. A lot. I'd have to be satisfied with that, sinking back down on the cushions as footsteps bounded down the hall. For now.

***

The clang of weights was starting to give me a headache. After Kiernan and Jade took off, I'd hit the gym. The one located in the east end of the first floor.

Jeez, I lived in a house with an 'east end', how pompous did that sound?

Usually I preferred the public gym. More people, more distractions. But I wasn't feeling particularly social. Lack of sleep made me cranky, so I was keeping to myself. For the safety of others.

I did have one stop on my to-do list for the day, though. The auto parts store. I could have just taken my baby to the shop. I was by no means a qualified mechanic, but a friend of mine from back home—or back where home *used to be*—had taught me a thing or two about cars. He'd always insisted that if I got lazy and let money take care of what I could do myself, it would have been a waste of his time. We wouldn't want that. Plus, getting under the hood of a car was about the best way I could think of to reclaim my manhood after my recent delve into the lifestyles of Martha Stewart. Therefore, despite the fact that it was as cold as a penguin's ass in January, the new air filter was going in today.

Dropping the barbell back in its cradle, I reached for a towel to wipe the sweat stinging my eyes. I'd done enough. My arms were starting to feel watery and it wasn't safe to continue without a spotter.

After a quick rinse in the shower, I was coasting down Main Street looking for an open parking spot. The only available one was outside the jewelry store. A small place, locally owned, with a lot of unique, one-of-a-kind pieces. It's not like I spent a lot of time perusing diamond earrings and platinum bracelets, but I took the occasional peek when I passed by. Some of their stuff was incredible. Too bad I had no one to buy it for.

Today was no different. The absurd sapphire hanging on display caught my attention and suckered me right in. The giant thing was encrusted in diamonds and looked ridiculously like something right out of *Titanic*. Money generally wasn't a major concern for me, but even I cringed at the thought of the price tag attached.

"Like that, you should see some of the stuff they have *inside*."

ANGEL

Startled—and somewhat embarrassed to be caught scoping out women's jewelry—I twisted around to find Marjorie examining the necklace beside me.

"Hey. What are you doing here?"

"Shopping." She hefted the multiple bags dangling from her arms like that should have been some sort of clue. "What's it look like?"

Marjorie wasn't the . . . warmest person I'd ever met, but I was getting a particularly frigid vibe from her today.

"Come and look." She opened the door and stood there holding it, not giving me much of a choice but to accompany her inside.

She wasn't wrong. The sheer variety alone was impressive. Not everything was as gaudy as the stuff they put on display. Some of it was actually quite . . . elegant.

"So, are you shopping for someone . . . *special*?"

And why did that sound like it had a whole lot of hidden meaning behind it?

"No. No one special." No one, at all.

"Oh, silly me. Here, I thought you'd grown half a brain since shooting Beth down." Marjorie tipped her head back to glare up at me, not intimidated in the slightest by the massive size difference between us.

"I didn't shoot her down, Marjorie." And I didn't have the patience for this. "I'm just—"

"Busy. Yeah. So I've heard."

"Exactly."

"Sounds like a copout to me." With barely a glance around, she headed back toward the door. "Just in case you work out your issues . . . She's got a thing for rubies."

"Okay." But rubies were the furthest thing from my mind as the door jingled shut behind her.

All of my thoughts centered on a single piece hanging behind glass on the wall.

"Is there something I can help you with?" A woman bustled out from the back room, wiping her hands on the front of her jeans. "So sorry. I was just eating lunch."

"No . . ." My brain was operating in slow-mo, most of its power diverted to trying to convince me to let it go. But I'd zeroed in on it and it was

like the rest of the world just disappeared. It was
. . . perfect. "It's okay."

I really did try to ignore it. To forget about it.
Walk away and leave it alone. It wasn't my place
to be giving her pretty things. But as I watched
the store clerk box the sparkling, silver angel
wing pendant and handed her my credit card, I
convinced myself that it was *for* Jade, not *from*
me.

It didn't matter who paid for it. She deserved
to have it.

Sixteen

Hypnotizing flames flickered as a familiar warmth wrapped around my gooseflesh. I was the first one up Christmas morning, so I'd shuffled downstairs like some kind of zombie to get a fire started in the living room. Not as impressive as it sounds.

I would've loved to have built the thing from scratch. Stacking the wood just right, feeding the flames, giving them room to breathe and grow. I could do it. I used to love camping along the coast with my friends. We'd spend entire weekends on the shore hanging out, talking, listening to music, maybe drinking a little. We used to build bonfires on the sand. Burning entire tree branches. Seeing how high we could coax the flames.

Here, all I had to do was flip a switch.

ANGEL

Sinking onto the sofa, I watched them dance and play. Allowing them to draw me back to a place I usually avoided going. I missed the pops and cracks of real wood. The hum of familiar voices. The shouts and laughter and the sand between my toes. Everything had seemed so easy back then. Like life had been handed to me on a silver platter to enjoy.

Then, Kiernan was diagnosed. And I realized that platter could be snatched away as quickly as it was given. My friends no longer knew how to be around me. They didn't know what to say, what to do, how to act. Neither did I.

Nothing was easy anymore.

The ceiling above me creaked. Kiernan was moving around his room. It took some effort to shake the melancholy that was quietly creeping over me, but I did it. It was Christmas. And it was going to be the best damn Christmas any of us had ever seen.

The kitchen was Mom's domain. Generally, you entered at your own risk, but today, I thought it worth it. Pulling out a frying pan, a few bowls, and a wire whisk, I cracked a dozen eggs, chopped some broccoli, peppers, onions, and ham, and threw in some butter and milk. You didn't live with my mother your whole life and not learn a thing or two about cooking.

"Mmm. What's that smell?" Kiernan's arms were extended high overhead as he arched his back into a stretch.

"Farmer's omelets. Want one?" I slid the spatula under the fluffy eggs and wiggled my first masterpiece onto a plate.

"Is that a question?"

No. It really wasn't. The plate landed in front of Kiernan without waiting for an answer. I dumped the next batch into the pan while he snagged a fork from the cutlery drawer and plopped down at the kitchen table.

"Mms ss elly ood." He sounded like he was speaking some alien language through the massive bite he was trying to chew and swallow at the same time, but I could hear a compliment when I got one.

"Thanks. Is Mom up?"

"Yeah. She's in the shower."

Good to know. I was using her stove, the least I could do was have a yummy breakfast ready to appease her wrath when she found out. The concoction bubbled and solidified in the pan.

ANGEL

The scent alone had my stomach growling by the time the second omelet was done, but I set it aside for Mom and moved onto the third.

"What are you two up to in here?" She stood near the doorway, frowning at the raw egg and wrappers scattered across her counter.

"Making breakfast. Here." I handed her the plate by way of a peace offering.

"*Cal's* making breakfast. I'm just eating it." Kiernan managed to throw me under the bus from clear across the room.

"Thanks a lot, bro. Merry Christmas to you, too."

Kiernan grinned and shrugged as Mom took her meal to join him.

"Well, since your brother did all the cooking, it seems only fair that you should do the cleaning." Mom smiled brightly at Kiernan and if my hands weren't covered in melted butter, I would have high-fived her. "I expect this room to shine before a single present gets opened."

Kiernan slumped in his seat and stifled a groan by shoving his last bite in that big mouth of his.

I definitely made out on the deal. It took him nearly twice as long to clean the mess as it took me to make it. I listened to him grumble about me being a 'slob', wiping counters, washing dishes, and reshelving ingredients, while I sat back and enjoyed my eggs, which—notably—turned out as good as they smelled.

***

Mom was a big believer in celebrating, but she wasn't a big believer in 'stuff'. Yes, we had a lot more stuff than most people, but to her that was just another reason why we didn't need more. Made sense. How were we supposed to appreciate anything we had if it was constantly being replaced? Gifts were light. Some books I needed for school, a few I actually *wanted* to read, new clothes, concert tickets, and a stack of video games and movies.

I was pretty excited about our haul. Especially the concert tickets, though I had no idea who I was supposed to give the second one to. But what really had me on the edge of my seat was what came next.

Jade—and her *mother*—were one their way over.

To our house.

ANGEL

This was going to prove interesting.

During my first encounter with the woman, I hadn't exactly been paying a lot of attention to *her*. Over time, I'd built her up to be this giant evil beast of a woman with claws, fangs, and a razor sharp tongue. But she wasn't. At least not on the outside.

Her outer appearance actually resembled Jade very closely. Only older and more worn. The way I feared Jade would someday look if her life continued the way it had been. But things seemed different now.

She was ushered inside through a whirlwind of hugs and greetings, where Kiernan deposited her on the couch across from me, immediately claiming the seat beside her. "Sit down. I want to give you your presents."

"Presents?" Jade hugged a shoulder bag to her chest as she glanced around the room and her eyes bulged at the stack of gifts awaiting her under the tree.

They weren't all from Kiernan. Having only two sons, Mom didn't have cause to buy girlie things very often. I was guessing she'd had a field day at the mall. My cheeks ached, trying to hold back a smile. Finally, Jade was getting something she deserved.

Her mother hovered in the doorway, looking nervous and embarrassed. It seemed just deserts were on the menu for the day. Until Jade took pity on her.

"Mom, will you sit with me?"

There was a flash of anger as I watched the relief wash over Marilyn's face. I must have had a serious problem if someone's kindness towards another person was enough to piss me off, but Jade's mother was the last person on Earth to deserve it. Especially, from Jade.

But that didn't matter to her. She really was an Angel.

"Are you all just going to sit around watching me?" A dark flush crept into Jade's cheeks, settling into a warm burn that cast off more heat than the fireplace.

The smile had vanished from her face and her eyes darted anxiously from one person to the next.

When they reached me, I smirked at her. "Yes. So you'd better get to it, or it's going to be a boring show."

ANGEL

"Cal!" Task accomplished. All eyes turned to us as Mom smacked my arm. I could have sworn I even heard Jade chuckle before she tore into her first present.

When she'd finished opening everything from Kiernan and Mom, and thanked them both a zillion times, I still hadn't decided what to do with the tiny box tucked neatly away in my pocket. I couldn't just whip it out and hand it to her in front of everyone. And the fact that I felt the need to hide it spoke volumes toward the foolishness of giving it to her at all.

In the end, I decided to make as little of it as possible. I didn't need to see her face when she opened it. And I didn't need her thanks. She didn't even need to know who it was from. Though the angel wing would probably give that much away.

I waited until she retreated upstairs with Kiernan and dug her jacket out of the closet. Zipping it into the pocket, I left it for her to find. That way she wouldn't feel pressured to wear it, or even keep it, if it made her uncomfortable.

They were gone for a long time. Hours without resurfacing. I thought Mom would go up and check on them, but she didn't. If I'd taken a girl to my room in high school . . . *Yeah. No way*. But as we all knew, things were different for Kiernan. And evidently, Mom felt inclined to let him spend his Christmas any way he pleased.

Jade's mother, for the most part, seemed to be struggling just to keep up with my mother. Not a task I envied her. Mom was on a mission. When it came to holiday dinners, she was this multitasking super woman extraordinaire. You either kept up, or got run over.

I steered clear, spending most of the afternoon stretched out on the sofa, reading a new book.

Dinnertime didn't need to be announced. You could smell it. And it smelled . . . amazing.

Kiernan and Jade joined us in the dining room as we rearranged decorations to fit the gargantuan turkey Mom had baked to perfection, along with every side dish imaginable. Settled around the table, we started passing bowls until everyone's plates were filled to overflowing. Then, we dug in.

Food was not something we were shy about in our house. We could afford the good stuff, so we bought the good stuff. We cooked the good stuff. And we ate the good stuff. We *enjoyed* the good stuff. Not to unhealthy proportions—except maybe on holidays—but we didn't hold back.

Something both Jade and, strangely, her mother found very amusing. They watched us stuff our faces and then they laughed. *Both* of them. Something that seemed to surprise Jade as much as it did me.

"What's so funny?" Dropping my fork in a puddle of gravy, I sat back to watch them.

They laughed and smiled at each other. Jade looked so damn . . . happy. She was practically glowing. My ceaseless prayers for Kiernan took a backseat for a moment as I offered up a new one.

Please, let this work. Please, let this be her life from now on. Let her be happy. Please . . . just let her be happy.

But I'd been praying for a really long time without answer.

"Dinner was fantastic, Claire. Thank you." When the meal was over, Marilyn stood, collecting Jade's plate along with her own and rounded the table. "Can I help you with cleanup?"

"That would be great. Thanks." Mom gathered a few empty bowls and headed into the kitchen.

A heavy sadness crept over Jade, weighing her shoulders and her smile down, as she watched them go.

"You okay?" Kiernan had noticed it, too.

"Yeah. I just . . . I don't know . . . It's just . . . Too good to be true, ya know? Like . . . Like . . ." She seemed unsure what she was trying to say, but I knew exactly what she was feeling.

"You keep waiting for the other shoe to drop?" Because I'd felt it, too. Too many times to count.

She caught my eye and I knew she felt it, the understanding between us. The recognition of shared fears and disappointments.

"Yeah. Like this can't possibly last. This can't possibly be my life and I should hang on to it for as long as I can."

"Good things do happen, Jade." Kiernan's lips pressed into a flat line as he scooted closer to hers. "It's okay to have hope."

"But what if . . ."

"You dare to hope and it's taken away?" I knew what that felt like, too. Every single time they'd started Kiernan on a new drug, recommended a new therapy, I'd had that rising tide of hope wash over me. And every time the therapy failed, every time the drugs were ineffective, I felt that wave of utter heartbreak and disappointment crash down.

The look Kiernan shot me warned that I was on dangerous ground. "You can't be afraid to hope, Jade. Life without hope . . . That's not life. Trust me."

He was *guilting* her into having hope. A low-handed move to begin with. But when that fragile hope hinged on an addict's ability to stay sober . . .

"You're right. I should be thankful for what I have and not waste it being afraid that I may lose it."

"There's my girl." Kiernan cupped her chin, running his thumb over the cheek of 'his girl'. *His* girl. And she closed her eyes to savor *his* touch.

My stomach felt heavy, as though I'd eaten one too many helpings of mashed potatoes and gravy. Extracting myself from their private moment, I went upstairs to lie down and digest.

***

I woke with a sudden start, stunned that I'd actually fallen asleep. Stretching out a kink in my neck, I went in search of anyone who could tell me what I'd missed. The house was quiet. The only sounds coming from where Kiernan's bedroom door hadn't quite shut all the way.

Muffled, tear-filled sobs.

Angling myself to the gap, I saw him clutching something to his chest as he cried his eyes out.

He'd cried a few times in the beginning, though not as much as you'd expect. He'd cried for the fight ahead of him, the pain, the loss of our father . . . but this time was different. There had always been something buried beneath his grief in the past. Hope, helping him to hold on, giving him strength. That was gone now. He no longer cried for a difficult future, but the lack of one. His sorrow was all encompassing, and it swamped me.

I felt it, too. The significance of the sun setting outside his window. The end of what would be his last Christmas. And it cut deep. My soul felt brittle. Worn too thin and on the verge of shattering. But I didn't have that luxury. Kiernan needed me. He needed me to be strong for him. To lend him my strength when he lacked his own. So, I slapped on another layer of duct tape and crazy glue, and held it together.

"Hey." The door swung open wider on my knock and I watched Kiernan scramble to shove a notebook under his comforter as I stepped into the room. "It's just me."

"Oh . . . Um . . . Hey. I was just . . ." He swiped at the tears trickling down his cheeks and I ignored the ones still gleaming in his eyes.

"It's okay. We don't have to talk about it." Not talking was better than listening to him lie to me. He was hurting. He knew it and I knew it. We both knew why. And we both knew there was nothing either of us could do about it. So what else was there to talk about, anyway?

I sat on his mattress beside him and waited. He struggled against it, but there was no stopping the tears in his eyes from falling. And when he surrendered, I wrapped my arm around his shoulders and I held him. I held onto him while he cried. While he got it all out. And I took it all in.

I took his heartbreak, his rage, his terror of the unknown. I let it sink inside of me, beneath the armor and the walls. I let it eat at me. Strangle me. Tear me apart.

Because it was better me, than him.

I could take it.

The sun sank and darkness filled the room long before Kiernan finished. Wiping the tears on his sleeve, he twisted to stare out his blackened window.

"You can't tell her not to have hope, Cal."

I wasn't surprised that we were pretending the previous hour never happened. I *was* surprised that this was how we were going to do it. "I wasn't telling her not to have hope. I was warning her not to get her hopes *up*."

"Why shouldn't she?" Kiernan shifted to face me again, and though still red and puffy, the sadness in his eyes had been replaced with something else. Anger. "You saw her mom. She's doing really well. Things are good for her. *Finally*. She should enjoy that. She deserves to."

"I'm not arguing that. But what if you're wrong? What if everything comes crashing down? There's nothing worse than false hope."

"Yes. There is. *No* hope. I've seen that look in her eyes before, the hopelessness. I won't let you put it back there. Everything's going to be fine."

"And what if it's not?"

"It *is*."

"What if it isn't?"

"*It is!* It has to be." Because he wouldn't be around to pick up the pieces if things fell apart again. "You don't care about her. You don't care about anyone. All you care about is getting to play the damn hero. You *enjoy* watching everyone else's lives turn to shit just so you can swoop in and save the goddamn day. She doesn't need you. Stay the hell away from her."

I was on my feet, backing toward the door with Kiernan right in my face. The moment I cleared the threshold, he slammed it hard enough to knock the picture of the two of us hanging on the wall to the floor. The frame cracked, but I couldn't have cared less.

Across the hall, I sat on my bed, fisting the sheets and counted to ten. And then twenty. And then . . . I'd reached a hundred before there was a knock at the door. I didn't have to open it to know who it was. Or what he wanted. Kiernan had come to apologize. Just like he always did. That was how this went.

His mood shifts were becoming more and more common. Whether a direct side effect of the tumor pressing on the personality center of his brain or a culmination of the constant stress he was under finally breaking free, I wasn't sure. All I knew was that he'd lash out at the safest thing he could, which happened to be me more times than not. And then he'd apologize for it.

That last bit was unnecessary. If anyone was overdue a meltdown or two, it was Kiernan. I was a big boy.

I could take it.

Seventeen

He hit the ground like a ton of bricks. One minute we were laughing about our serious need to practice some of the new games we'd gotten for Christmas, and the next he was twitching and jerking on the living room floor.

"Kiernan!" I dropped down beside him and had to forcibly stop myself from reaching out. Any type of restraint during a seizure could seriously hurt him. "Mom!"

Violent muscle spasms wracked his body, jolting him clear off the floor. "*Mom!*"

Footsteps thundered down the stairs. "Cal? Oh, my God. I'm calling 9-1-1."

She bolted for the kitchen, while Kiernan continued to convulse, spittle flying from his mouth. All of the color drained from his face. His lips turned an unnatural shade of purple. And his eyes . . . they rolled back into his head until all I could see were two white, veined orbs.

"Kiernan? Kiernan, dammit, you fight! You hear me? Don't you dare give up on me. Kiernan!"

Oh, my God.

Oh, my God.

Please.

Please, no.

Not now.

Not yet.

"Kiernan!" The force of holding back the hysterics building up inside of me was tearing up my throat like jagged glass, causing an ache to rival the one in my chest. "Kiernan, please. Hold on. Just hold on. The ambulance is coming. Please. It's almost over. Just hang on. It's almost over."

'Almost' turned out to be nearly seven minutes long. Seven minutes that felt like seven lifetimes. And when it was over . . . When he lay there limp, unconscious, and wrung-out, I thought . . . I was so sure . . .

ANGEL

"Pease. Please, no. Not yet." The broken plea fell from my trembling lips. "Not yet, dammit! *Not yet!*"

I wasn't ready. This couldn't be it. I couldn't even remember what the last thing I'd said to him was.

My hands fisted in my hair, tugging painfully at the roots. "Kiernan. You can't go. Not like this. You can't—"

I saw it. The gentle rise and fall of his chest.

An animalistic sound I didn't even realize I was capable of making filled the room as I fell forward. On hands and knees, I crawled to my brother and brushed my fingers over the pulse point in his neck. Faint and thready, but it was there.

"He's alive." I meant to shout the words. Scream them to the Heavens. But after traversing the tattered wreckage of my throat, they came out as little more than a whisper.

Mom heard them, anyway. She flew past me to gather his head in her lap as I sank to my rear and watched them. Watched as her lips moved over quiet words of comfort. Watched her shaky fingers comb through his unruly hair. Watched her cradle her baby in her arms. All the while, telling myself over and over again that he was alive.

My little brother was still alive.

For now.

Despite their noisy sirens and flashy lights, EMTs don't actually move all that fast. Busy gathering equipment and organizing paperwork, I couldn't help thinking if it was their kid laid out on the floor, there might have been a little more pep in their step. Mom didn't exactly make things easier, refusing to release Kiernan. I had to literally hold her back while they hefted him onto the stretcher and into the back of the ambulance. But when Mom climbed in after them, I had no doubt they wouldn't be wasting any time getting to the hospital.

The mobile side-show screamed to life and I was at once grateful we didn't have any nearby neighbors. My heart told me to get in my car and follow them. Not to let that ambulance out of my sight for a moment. But my head reminded me I had one other stop to make along the way.

Gravel pinged against the undercarriage as my tire peeled out and I punched Jade's number into my cell.

ANGEL

"Cal?" She was scared. I hadn't even opened my mouth, yet, and she was already frightened.

"Jade, are you at home?" I needed to get to her. To be with her. I couldn't think about anything else.

"Yeah. Wh—?"

"I'm coming to get you. Meet me outside."

"What happened?"

That was something I would have rather left unsaid until I could do it in person, but I'd already stirred the pot just by calling her. I couldn't leave her hanging until I got there. "Kiernan had another seizure. They took him to the hospital."

Neither of us were strangers to Kiernan's seizures. We'd both witnessed them before, but this one just *felt* different. Maybe it was brotherly intuition. Maybe I'd been subconsciously picking up on changes in him for a while and part of me had been expecting this. I don't know. Maybe it was the universe, trying to warn me about what was coming next. As though that could possibly make up for any of this.

"Angel?" I don't know *how* I knew. I simply *knew.* "It's bad."

***

I drove like a raging lunatic the whole way to the hospital. I probably should have stopped. Or, at the very least, slowed down. Hell, I should have let Jade drive. She didn't even have her license, but she couldn't have put us in any more danger than I had.

It didn't seem to bother her. There was no backseat driving, no grabbing for the handle bar. In fact, she leaned forward in her seat the entire way, straining against her seatbelt as though that would somehow get us there faster.

By some miracle, we made it to the hospital in one piece. Jade was prepared to continue the mad dash straight through the front doors, but I shackled her wrist before she could escape the car.

"Angel . . . You heard me, right? This morning when he . . ." Memories of that god-awful scene would continue to haunt me for the rest of my life. "It's bad, Jade."

"He's had seizures before. I saw him have one and it looked really bad, but he was—"

"This is different. This time . . ." This time I knew what was coming. I'd always imagined that losing Kiernan would be the greatest pain I'd ever have to suffer, but now I *knew* it. If only for a fraction of a second, I'd endured it. Felt the loss of a future that was never meant to be. Cheering him on as he crossed that stage on graduation day, having him stand beside me at my wedding, spoiling my nieces and nephews. Games, vacations, family barbeques. Things that were doomed to failure. Nonsense notions that led to nothing but disappointment and bitterness.

My knuckles cracked when they collided with the steering wheel, but it didn't hurt nearly as bad as hearing Jade yelp beside me like a kicked puppy.

"I'm sorry. I'm . . ." I was such an idiot. She gaped at me across the car with wide, frightened eyes. I was screwing this up. Probably one of the most important things I'd do in my entire life, and I was already screwing it up. "You just . . . You need to be prepared because . . . I don't know if he's coming home this time."

There, I'd said it. Put voice to my greatest fear. And hers.

Tears flooded Jade's eyes, but she blinked them all away before a single one fell. "Cal?"

"Angel?" My entire body vibrated with raw need. I *needed* her. God, how I needed her.

"We can do this." Her nose twitched as she sniffled back the last of her tears. Her tiny chin lifted a fraction of an inch and she looked me right in the eye. "We can do this. For Kiernan."

Strength and courage poured off of her and I soaked it in. She was giving that to me. Giving me what I needed most, the ability to support the people I loved. And, right that moment, I loved her for it.

"You're right. We can do this. We *have* to do this."

"Where's your mom?"

"She's inside. She rode in the ambulance with Kiernan."

"Alright." She gave a gentle tug and I released her so she could finally open her door. "Let's go find out what's going on, and take it from there. One step at a time, okay?"

"One step at a time." Maybe I *could* do this, if I looked at it only one moment to the next. With Jade by my side, maybe I could do anything. "Alright. Let's go."

Mom looked like something right out of the Walking Dead. Her hair was a knotted nest of snares and tangles. Her makeup painted her face in shades of blue and black and gray. It ran and smeared in random patterns until she looked like a walking, talking piece of abstract art.

"Mrs. Parks?" Jade approached with caution. She was timid and as fragile as the rest of us felt, but she took that first step. And it freed my feet from the cement shoes they'd been encased in, allowing me to do the same.

"Oh, Jade. Cal. You made it."

"Where is he?" I took Mom's arm and escorted her away from the desk, where a line was beginning to form, to find a place to sit.

"They're looking at him now. They won't tell me anything. They just keep saying—"

I knew what they kept saying. The same things they always said. "You know how this works, Mom. They do the same thing every time. No use making yourself crazy over it."

Hollow words coming from the complete basket case I was. It was true, this was just like every other time. Except . . . it wasn't. And I wasn't sure I could handle that.

"Hey, Cal." Jade glanced over my shoulder at something near the far wall. "Why don't you get us all some coffee, while your mom and I make a run to the bathroom?"

"I don't think I—"

"If anyone comes with news, I'll come get you right away." I knew what Mom was afraid of, but I wasn't about to let her pass up this opportunity. She was in desperate need of a moment to regroup. And, truthfully, so was I.

"See? It's okay. Come on." Jade took her arm and eased her from the chair like you would an elderly person. "Come with me. We'll only be a minute."

Mom looked like one, shuffling down the hall beside her. I watched them go. Angel never once let go of her arm.

Three paper cups sat on the floor by my feet, while I rubbed at the ache in the back of my neck. The coffee machine was out of milk, and creamer, and sugar, and pretty much everything else. I hoped Jade didn't mind drinking it black.

Mom more closely resembled a human being when they returned from the ladies room. She even managed to force a smile onto her face as she accepted her cup. And then, we did the only thing we could do.

ANGEL

We waited.

***

My phone battery was nearly dead from how often I'd turned it on just to check the time before a doctor finally came to talk with us.

"Mrs. Parks?"

"Yes." We all stood to greet the short, blonde woman in the white coat. "Yes, I'm Mrs. Parks. And this is my son. And my daughter."

Jade gasped and I wanted to reach out and squeeze her. She was a part of our family. *Permanently*. I hoped like hell that she knew nothing could ever change that.

"Let's have a seat, shall we?"

We sat and she talked. The longer she talked, the dizzier I felt. I don't know when all the medical mumbo-jumbo stopped sounding like a foreign language and started to make sense, but it did. And I was right.

Things were worse.

Things were a *lot* worse.

At some point, I reached out and held on to Jade. I didn't think about it, I just did it. She probably had no idea what we were talking about, but I needed to hold on to something. And she was it.

"He's been moved upstairs to a private room and he can have visitors, but I must insist on only one at a time."

Jade stiffened beside me and I knew what she was thinking. I felt it growing inside of her. That vicious, twisted, pitiless thing called 'hope'.

Eighteen

"You know this doesn't change anything, right?"

Mom had gone with the doctor to see Kiernan, leaving Jade and I alone in yet another waiting room. At least this one was private. No crying children. No old men hacking up a lung in your lap. Just me, and Jade, and silence so loud it was deafening.

"What I said in the car—"

"He's awake, Cal. She said he's awake."

"Yes, she did." It was probably the cruelest thing that had come out of the doctor's mouth. "But did you hear what else she said? Did you understand any of it?"

"Not really."

"She agrees that this time is worse. That Kiernan is worse."

"Did she say he won't get better?"

"No. Of course not. She can't say that because she can't know that." And because medicine is essentially a business. One that thrives and feeds on false hope. I wanted to be a doctor, but I swore to myself right then that I would never, ever sugarcoat anything for anyone. People needed to know the truth. No matter how painful it was.

"Then neither can you." Jade was in denial. A dangerous place to be. Instead of bracing herself for the truth, preparing for impact, she was going to be blindsided by it.

"Angel . . ." All of my energy seemed to abandon me at once. It would have been easy to let it go. To stop arguing and let Jade tell herself whatever she wanted to. But that would have been crueler than making her hear me. "I'm not saying this to upset you. And I'm not telling you not to have hope. I'm just trying to warn you that this may not turn out the way everyone wants it to. I know there's no way to prepare for that. I've been trying to find a way for a year. It doesn't exist. But there will come a time when we have to face it. And if that time came, and caught you off-guard . . . I'd never forgive myself."

"Okay."

Okay, my ass. I could *see* her reinforcing those walls around her heart, refusing to let my words sink in.

Mom's return was the first blow to Jade's barricade of denial. She staggered into the room, pale faced, with this distant stare that I doubt even saw us sitting there. She looked . . . defeated.

I felt the emotional strike it dealt. Felt the reverberations shudder through Jade's body.

Her gaze was fixated on Mom, horrified by what she saw, what it meant, yet unable to look away. Feeling some of that strength return— some of that strength *she'd* given me—I turned her to look at me, instead.

"Hang in there, Angel. You want to go next?"

"No." She sucked in a deep lungful and shook her head. "You're his brother. You should go."

"Are you sure?" The color was beginning to drain from her own face. Maybe if she talked to him . . . "I can wait if you want to see him."

"I'm okay. You go."

It was a physical effort to force myself out of that chair. I was no more ready to face this than she was, but time wasn't standing still and we couldn't afford to waste a single second of it.

I'd only made it halfway to standing before Jade's warm fingers wrapped around my wrist, pulling me back down. "We can do this, right?"

Brushing away some of the silky smooth strands from her face, I found the ability to smile at her. We had this weird symbiotic relationship. Each of us feeding off of whoever happened to be stronger. At the moment, that was me again. "Yeah, Angel. We can do this."

"The open door on the left." Mom's voice was robotic. She pointed down the hallway behind her without even looking at me.

"Mom?"

"Go. Talk to your brother." She continued forward toward Jade and I let her go, trusting an Angel to watch over one member of my family, while I went to check on the other.

The room was cold. Not just temperature wise, but a bone deep chill of foreboding crept over me as I stepped inside.

ANGEL

Kiernan was lying in one of those stiff, mechanical beds with the stupid side railings. Like sick people were too dumb to remember how not to fall off their mattress. It's not that I'd never seen him in one before, but this time there were cords and wires still attached to him that were normally removed before we were allowed into the room. Cords and wires I doubted deep in my gut would ever be removed.

"Hey, bro. How are you feeling?"

He struggled to sit up straighter as I crossed the room.

"I'm fi—" He took a second look at me and rethought his answer. "I'm tired. I feel really, really tired."

He looked it, too. In fact, he looked a lot like Mom. *Defeated*. I wondered if I looked the same. But Kiernan would never really be defeated. He couldn't be. He'd fought so hard for so long . . . No matter what the outcome, he'd already won. Each and every day since his diagnosis had been a victory. And to the victor went the spoils. In this case, the spoils might just be some long overdue peace.

"Do you want to rest? I can . . ." I hooked my thumb toward the door, but Kiernan shook his head.

"No. Stay. There's something I have to talk to you about."

"Okay." I pulled up the chair beside his bed and settled in. "What's up?"

"What you said the other day . . . at Jade's . . . about being there for her. Did you mean it?"

"What?"

"Did you mean it?"

"Yes. Of course I meant it. Where is this coming from, Kier?"

"I just . . . I need to know. I need to know she's going to be alright. I *have* to."

"She'll be alright."

His eyes met mine and though he'd been struggling to keep them open only moments before, his gaze held steady. "Swear it."

"Kiernan—"

"Swear it, Cal. *Swear* you'll take care of her. *Swear* you'll be there for her. She's stronger than she thinks, but I don't want to leave her alone. No one should be all alone. Swear you'll protect her. Even from herself. That you won't let anything bad happen to her. *Swear*, Cal. Please."

I looked into my brother's watery eyes and saw the fear behind the sorrow. He was so afraid. My little brother was terrified, and there was very little I could do to make it better.

So I did what I could. I swore.

And it sickened me to my soul that I didn't do it entirely for him.

"Thanks, bro." Some of the more immediate panic eased away and he settled back onto the hard pillow. "Do you think you could send her in here? I really need to talk to her."

"Of course. I'll go get her. You rest."

"Thanks, Cal." Kiernan reached out and grabbed my arm as I rose to go. His grip was so weak, I wanted to grab his hand and hold it, and promise to never leave his side. "Cal? I mean it. Thank you. For everything. I know what you've done. I know you stepped up when Dad left. I know you gave up everything to move here. I know I put you through hell."

"Kiernan, you never—"

"And you never once complained. You never got mad. You could have left, too. You could have gone away to college. You could have stayed at home with your friends. But you didn't. All you've done for the past year-and-a-half has been for me and Mom. I know I didn't always act like it, but . . . I wanted you to know that I know it. And that it means more than you can ever know."

My little brother—the one human being on the planet that it was my duty to protect—laid in that damn hospital bed, staring up at me through tear-filled eyes. He was fighting a losing battle. I was watching him get pummeled and there wasn't a damn thing I could do about it. I wanted to reach inside his body and tear out that tumor with my bare hands. Stand between it and him, and refuse to let it have him. Not *my* brother. I wanted to beg it to take me, instead. There was so much more Kiernan could do in this life. More than I could ever hope to. He had people who counted on him. Who *needed* him. I was nobody. Lost. Confused. Angry. Nothing. Why was it fair that I lived when he didn't get to?

Then he did the most unexpected thing. Kiernan threw his arms around my waist and he hugged me. He hugged me with all of his strength and he must have borrowed some of mine, as well, because my legs gave out and I sank down to kneel on the floor beside his bed. Memories of him as a snot-nosed kid, running around, driving me mad, played through my mind as he buried his face in my neck.

I didn't say anything. I couldn't think of anything *to* say. I was speechless. So I just held onto him as hot tears soaked my skin.

"You're my hero, Cal."

No. His words tore through me like a razor blade. Anger welling fast in their wake. No, dammit, I was no one's hero. I was a failure. As a brother. As a son. As a friend. I'd failed. All of them.

"You've got that backward, little brother. *You're* the hero here." A shudder that I couldn't suppress wracked my body. "I love you, Kiernan."

"I love you, too, Cal."

***

When I left his room, I knew. I knew I'd seen my brother for the last time. Spoken to him for the last time. Touched him . . . for the last time.

I went straight to the closest bathroom, locked the door, braced myself against the cold porcelain sink, and I breathed. Anything more, anything less, and I wouldn't have survived. So I just breathed. The scent of piss and Clorox filled my nose, and still I breathed. Deeply. Again and again. Reminding myself that I could.

I was going to survive this day. Life was going to go on from here. I just couldn't see how other than one moment at a time. The first of which included getting Jade into that room where Kiernan was waiting for her.

I startled her when I stepped into the waiting room, and she stared up at me with this crushing combination of hope and dread. Her shields were up, but they were practically transparent. "How are you feeling?"

She took a moment to think that over. A range of emotions flickered over her face, but the one she settled on was, "Helpless."

There wasn't a more perfect word in any language to accurately describe exactly how this felt. "Yeah. Me, too. Are you ready?"

"Yeah." Bullshit. She was nowhere close to 'ready'. None of us were. "I'm ready."

ANGEL

"Last door on the left." But whether or not we were ready, this was going to happen. "And, Jade?"

"Yeah?"

"Take a breath before you open the door."

It was pointless. I was trying to prepare her for something I, myself, wasn't prepared for. Something there was no way to prepare for. We were all about to hit a brick wall, head-on. And we were going to do it full speed ahead.

***

"Caulder?"

I blinked and realized I'd been staring at nothing for what felt like a long time. Mom was sitting beside me and I hadn't even seen her come in.

"Mom. Where were you?"

"In the bathroom." All of her makeup had been washed off, but I doubted that was what made her look a million years older all of a sudden. "I called your father."

"What did he say?" Nothing I wanted to hear, I was sure.

"Not much. He was late for a meeting."

"He was late for a—?" That useless piece of—

"He can't deal with this, Cal. He's made that perfectly clear from the beginning. He can't think about it. He can't talk about it. Your father loves Kiernan. He loves both of you. Very much. He's just—"

"Weak." The man was a spineless coward.

Mom sighed. "Yes. He's weak. He's a kind, gentle man, but he's fragile. He's only trying to protect himself the only way he knows how."

"And what about us? Isn't it his job to protect us?"

"You're right." Her lips pressed into a thin line and she nodded. "It is his job. And mine. I'm sorry, Cal. I'm sorry I didn't make a better choice for you both. I'm sorry I didn't fight harder to—"

"No. Mom. This is *not* your fault." And I'd be damned if I'd let her shoulder his guilt along with what she already carried. "Nothing Dad did is your fault. He's a grown man. He makes his own decisions. Kiernan and I . . . We don't need him. We are so lucky just to have you. You're more than enough for us. Just you."

ANGEL

"Oh, Cal." Tears streamed down her cheeks as she squeezed my hand between two of hers. "I don't say this nearly enough, but I am so, so proud of you. Of the man that you've become. You are so much stronger than your father. I'm sorry that you've had to be."

"Don't be. I want to make you proud."

We lapsed into silence after that. Hands still entangled between us, we sat side-by-side. And we waited. For the inevitable. And yet, when it came, it still took us both by surprise.

It started with the high-pitched peal of feedback through the speakers in the ceiling, followed by a voice announcing some kind of medical code. The sudden flow of bodies, wearing scrubs and lab coats, down the hall toward Kiernan's room stopped my heart. Maybe if I froze it right then, right that moment, it would never have to feel the moments that came after.

But it started up again and kicked into overdrive when I heard Jade screaming.

"No! No, Kiernan!" A large man in white scrubs was manhandling her out of the room, while she fought tooth and nail to break free. His muscles bulged and strained as he dragged her out into the hall and her small body raged and flailed hopelessly in his sturdy grasp.

"Get off her!" I'd body check the son of a bitch if he didn't let her go.

"She can't—"

"Get your hands off of her! *Now!*"

I don't know what he saw in my face, but it was enough to get him to release Jade and take a step back. Still hysterical, she was completely oblivious to my presence. I wrapped her up in my arms before she could get herself into trouble and held her tight.

"Shh, Angel. Hush. I've got you. I've got you."

I held her and I held *onto* her. Both of us holding the other up. I rocked her. And I whispered quiet words to her. And I tried not to think about why. Why she was screaming and sobbing. Why Mom stood beside us, both hands covering her open mouth. Why my legs felt like they were losing a battle with gravity. Why any of this was happening to us.

When some of the shock started to wear off, Jade gently extracted herself from my arms. I watched her wander past my mother as they both stared, captivated by the flurry of activity behind Kiernan's door. I couldn't do it. I didn't want to see what they were doing to him. I didn't want to know. I didn't want to know any of this. I didn't want to know this fear. This pain. This empty hollow ache forming deep inside my chest that I knew would never again feel whole.

But I did know. I knew exactly what was happening. Exactly how it felt. And I knew exactly when it was over. Mom's soul deep, anguished cry didn't signal the end of my pain, though. It only intensified it.

Her legs gave out and I was there, like I was always there. Giving her my strength when she needed it most. But there wasn't enough left to support us both. We went down, hard. Collapsing onto tile floor with Mom in my arms. Leaving Jade alone, with no one to lean on but herself.

There's one memory in everyone's life that stands out above the rest. One moment in time that's forever engrained in their hearts and minds. The sights, the sounds, the smells—all of it able to be recalled in flawless detail with a single thought. For some people it's prom night in the backseat of their parent's minivan with the homecoming queen. For other's it's scoring the winning goal. Holding their baby for the first time. The moment they looked into the eyes of the woman they loved and heard her say, 'I do.'

For me, that moment would forever be the look in Jade's eyes as she turned from us and walked away. The blank, glassy shield that couldn't quite hide the roiling turmoil underneath. I couldn't breathe, but somehow I found the air I needed to call her name.

I knelt in that hallway, holding one person that meant the world to me, watching the other walk away. Silently pleading with her to turn around. To come back and let me hold her, too. For her to hold me. I didn't know if that was what she wanted, but without a doubt, *she* was what *I* needed.

She didn't turn around. She didn't come back. She walked to the elevators at the end of the hall and boarded without so much as a glance in my direction.

As those shiny steel doors slid shut between us, I knew I'd lost more than my brother that day.

And it cracked my heart wide open.

***

ANGEL

I have only vague memories of taking Mom home after that. I probably shouldn't have been driving, but she couldn't and I wasn't thinking clearly enough to work out another way out of there. And that was all I wanted. To get the hell out of there.

There are glimpses of her taking some pills and putting her to bed. The slightest recollection of standing in the hallway outside her door until I was certain she'd fallen asleep. I don't remember walking to my room, at all. I don't remember crawling into bed. All I remember are the vivid dreams of drowning.

I was drowning.

Mom was drowning.

Jade was drowning.

The whole damn world was drowning.

Maybe that was because, in sleep, the last of my restraint shattered, and I cried enough tears to flood it.

~Not The End~

ACKNOWLEDGMENTS

A great big, giant THANK YOU to the amazing people without whom this book would not be what it is.

To the amazing, wonderful, beautiful people I have the pleasure of calling not only beta readers but friends: Cindy, Sherry, and Kendall.

To Kelsey of K Keeton Designs who took an amateur photo and turned it into a work of art. You are a magician, my friend. And she also happens to be an extremely talented photographer/ cover artist.

To the amazing fans who asked every day when this book would be released. It's your support and enthusiasm that keeps me doing what I'm doing. Every single email/message/ comment I receive from you fuels my passion and puts a huge grin on my face.

And last, but definitely not least, to the hubs, AKA my divine hand model for the cover image. *You* are *my* Angel.

ABOUT THE AUTHOR

Jamie Canosa is a full time author of YA/NA literature, which she absolutely loves. When she's not writing or spending time with her family, she can usually be found with her nose in a book. She currently resides in Upstate NY with her husband, and their three crazy kids . . . plus the cat, the bird, and the rabbit.

Learn more about Jamie at:
JamieCanosa.wix.com/author
https://www.facebook.com/AuthorJamieCanosa

Jade's story

continues in:

Pieces

OF MY HEART